LIGHTHOUSE TALES

BY

FREDERICK STONEHOUSE

Published by Avery Color Studios, Inc.
Gwinn, Michigan 49841

ISBN# 0-932212-99-9
Library of Congress Card No. 98-072282

June 1998

Cover Photo by:
Wayne S. Sapulski

TABLE OF CONTENTS

Chapter One

Lighthouses: The Early Years

General

*T*o fully understand the lighthouse tales that are the bulk of this book, the reader must have some appreciation of the role of the humble lighthouse in navigating the Great Lakes. The following overview is an attempt to provide enough information to place the stories into an acceptable historical context; to show how the lights developed and operated, the personalities and organizations integral to their success and afford an understanding of the broad applications of the equipment and devices used.

The first lighthouse built by the American colonists was established in 1716, at Little Brewster Island at the entrance to Boston Harbor. Others soon followed. Some were erected by cities, others by merchants. Providing lighthouses was not immediately perceived as a government responsibility. Following the American Revolution the control of the lights was retained by the individual states. After the 1789 constitution, lighthouses were centralized under the Treasury Department. By this time there were a dozen active beacons along the east coast.

On the Great Lakes, the first light reportedly was established in 1818, at Fort Niagara on Lake Ontario, although there is some debate in historical circles about this. It is possible the Presque Isle light on Lake Erie may have preceded it. Regardless of what station was the first on the lakes, by 1825 there were only four on the American side. After the Erie Canal opened that year, baring the lakes to immigration and commerce, the great flood began. Within four years the number of lights nearly doubled. In the decade of the 1830s, an additional 34 were constructed. At the beginning of the Civil War there were 102 on the lakes. Their placement supported the increased commerce. Where ships went, lighthouses soon followed. Each new light improved safety by warning mariners of dangerous shoals and reefs as well as guiding them to sheltered harbors. Initially the new lights were built on the shores of lakes Ontario and Erie. Later, as the new western lands opened up, new construction moved to Lakes Huron and Michigan. The first Lake Michigan lighthouse was placed at the entrance to the Chicago River in 1832.

Lake Superior was the last of the lakes to be developed. It was the discovery of iron ore and copper that sparked the great rush to the big lake. The first light was placed into service in 1849, although there is some confusion whether it was at Copper Harbor or at Whitefish Point since records indicate both were established at the same time. The 1855 opening of the St. Mary's Falls Ship Canal opened the flood gates of waterborne trade. By 1865 there were seven lighthouses on Lake Ontario, a dozen on Lake Huron, 26 on Lake Michigan and 15 on Lake Superior.

Ruins of the original Whitefish Point lighthouse. Credit: Michigan State Archives

Organization

The lights were initially placed under the Treasury Department in 1789, however, the department was unprepared to manage them. Responsibility for the lights became a hot potato within the department, bouncing between different offices. In 1820, it was finally given to Stephen Pleasonton, the Fifth Auditor, who also assumed the title of General Superintendent of Lights. He kept the potato for 32 years. His duties included administering contracts, responding to Congressional inquiries and generally overseeing the Lighthouse Service. Local customs collectors were given the additional job of superintending the lighthouses in their districts, including their operation and construction. In consideration of the extra work, they were given a 2.5 percentage commission on lighthouse disbursements. It was a thankless job for Pleasonton. A bookkeeper by profession, he had neither the maritime nor engineering background required to administer the duties in a competent manner. In addition, the position called for a man of iniative, great foresight and high management ability. He possessed none of these attributes, but instead seems to have been the perfect bureaucrat. He utterly failed to realize his responsibility for the lives of ship's crews and passengers and that he owed them the best navigational aids possible. He focused only on economy and never on quality. Witnesses reported he once stated he built lighthouses cheaper than anyone else and returned more money to the general fund than any other department. In all of the lighthouse literature, no one has a good word to say about Stephen Pleasonton.

While significant growth occurred during this period, overall management was very poor. The effort was generally to spend the least possible amount of money without regard to securing acceptable equipment or results. Contracts for construction and supplies and appointing keepers were based on political affiliation, not merit. There are many instances of poor construction as shown in the New Buffalo story. The outcome was a rising chorus of complaints from sailors, ship owners and insurers.

In 1837-38, Congress investigated the lighthouse operation and made a number of recommendations for improvement. Most of them Pleasonton ignored. Another Congressional inquiry was held in 1842, with more recommendations following. Pleasonton ignored them too!

Finally the complaints grew so loud that in 1851, Congress directed the Secretary of the Treasury to convene a special board to investigate the situation. The board's report was thorough and inclusive and concluded that the lighthouse establishment was poorly managed in both economy and efficiency. Keepers were ill-trained and in many cases incompetent and the lamps and reflectors were obsolete and inferior in design. During Pleasonton's reign the country's lighthouses were doubtless the worst in the civilized world.

Responding to the investigation, Congress in 1852 established through legislation a nine member Lighthouse Board with the Secretary of the Treasury as ex-officio president. Other members included scientists, U.S. Army Corps of Engineer officers, U.S. Navy officers and members of the U.S. Coast Survey. The new Board organized the lights into districts. In 1838, the Great Lakes were initially divided into two districts with the Detroit River as the boundary. The western district included Lakes Superior, Huron and Michigan while the eastern district included Lakes Erie and Ontario. In 1852, the lakes were reorganized. Lakes Ontario and Erie became the Tenth District and Lakes Superior, Huron and Michigan the Eleventh District. Another reorganization in 1886, divided the lakes into the Tenth District consisting of Lakes Erie and Ontario; the Ninth District, Lake Michigan; and the Eleventh, Lakes Superior and Huron. When in doubt, reorganize!

The Board also appointed an inspector for each district, giving him the responsibility of building and maintaining the lights and equipment as well as buying supplies. The inspector was required to inspect each station in the district once every three months. As the number of lights increased, additional help was provided for the inspector. An Army Corps of Engineer officer assisted with construction and maintenance duties. Local collectors of customs were kept on as lighthouse superintendents. They had the responsibility of appointing and paying keepers and handling routine fund disbursements. Eventually their role was phased out completely.

Central depots served as stationing locations for the lighthouse tenders and for storing and forwarding supplies. Repairs to the various apparatus were also accomplished there by specially trained craftsmen. Depots were located on the lakes at one time or another in Michigan at Detroit, St. Joseph, Charlevoix, and St. Marys River; in New York at Buffalo; in Pennsylvania at Erie; in Minnesota at Minnesota Point near Duluth and in Wisconsin at Milwaukee.

Improvements under the Board's leadership were significant. They established lights where needed and made certain they were well kept and reliable. Inefficient men were fired. The Board also experimented with new technology, trying whatever new equipment or fuels they thought might offer improvement. Before the advent of the Board, the US provided the worst lights in the advanced world. Under its management, they soon were the best. The Board also started a system of classifying lights based on the size of the lenses. The new method organized the lights into seven orders, with first order being the largest and seventh the smallest. Later the system would be changed to one based on candlepower.

Early lightkeepers often were selected based on political loyalties. Trustworthiness, reliability or competence were not requirements; political affiliation was. Congressmen with a light in their district didn't hesitate to use the appointment of a keeper as a real plum for a deserving bootlicker. Although the actual appointment of a keeper was the responsibility of the local collector of customs, these worthies were relatively far down the political food chain. Depending on the results of an election, wholesale dismissals and appointments were made. This happened so frequently that in the interest of efficiency and economy, the Lighthouse Board had blank forms printed to use when it was necessary to notify keepers that they had been replaced!

Watching the light! Credit: Author's Collection

Just because a keeper was of the right party and had a job didn't mean he was safe from efforts to remove him. Sometimes, "concerned citizens" would write letters to the Service complaining that the light started out the evening bright and clear, but that after a couple of hours it was extinguished. Obviously the keeper wasn't doing his job! Usually the writer offered to take his place.

The Lighthouse Board was well aware of the problem and tried its best to minimize the deleterious effect of politics and achieved some limited success. It did establish standards for the keepers to meet, which included a three month probationary period. After being tested on his duties by the district inspector or engineer, he could be dismissed for failure.

By the late 1870s, political appointments were largely confined to the entry level positions of a third or fourth assistant keeper at the bigger lights. The keeper or first assistant were generally career positions filled by cadre personnel.

After the Civil War it was common to see veterans appointed keepers as a reward for war service. In other instances the death of a keeper often resulted in the appointment of his wife or daughter as keeper, dependent on circumstance.

The Board worked hard to get or keep good men (or women). Vacancies usually occurred only by death, resignation or dismissal. The last was invariably due to drunkenness or failure to properly keep the light. The biggest cause of keeper loss was resignation. For example, between 1885—1889, the Lighthouse Board hired 1190 new keepers and 680, or well over half, resigned. The Board was steadfast in saying that the men were not leaving because of low pay, but more likely the result of isolation and the heavy demands of the job. Although a lightkeeper's pay was comparatively low, it was considerably more than a life-saving keeper received. In cases where the two stations were located next to one another, there was often a degree of contention between the two keepers. The life-saver, who regularly risked his life and those of his crew in the worst of storms, was paid less than the light keeper, who likely remained snug and safe in his nice warm lighthouse.

The Lighthouse Board, and later Bureau of Lighthouses, eventually established high standards for keepers and held them to the mark. Neither organization tolerated mistakes. They investigated and if necessary took appropriate action, including dismissal. Drunkenness, sleeping on duty or being absent from the station without authorization were considered major offenses and dismissal was a common penalty.

It wasn't until 1884 that uniforms were prescribed for keepers in an attempt to create a sense of pride among the men. The uniforms were intended for official or formal occasions, such as when the inspector made his "white glove" inspection or national holidays when visitors might be expected. The first one was given to the keepers. Afterwards they were expected to purchase uniform replacements as needed. For a while the men wore regular clothing on normal work days. Later the uniform requirement was extended to anytime the keeper was on duty.

The public outcry against the evils of the spoils system finally resulted in the passage by Congress in 1883 of the Pendleton Civil Service Act. Under it, appointments to key government positions would be based on ability, and special examinations were required of all applicants. Although initially only a few agencies were covered by the act, later presidents gradually increased the number. In 1896, President Cleveland added the U.S. Lighthouse Service and from then on appointments were based on merit. Following World War I, special consideration was often given to wounded veterans, a most laudable effort on behalf of those who so bravely served.

To increase efficiency, in 1903 the Service was transferred to the new Department of Commerce and Labor. During the period of rapid growth, the old Lighthouse Board system of management became too cumbersome. It was felt the jolt of moving to the new Commerce Department might rejuvenate it. It did not. In 1910 Congress abolished the Lighthouse Board and established in its stead the Bureau of Lighthouses. The new organization remained under the Commerce Department. Instead of the nine-member board, there was now only one man, the Commissioner of Lighthouses. From 1910—1935, the Commissioner was George R. Putnam, an experienced and energetic Coast and Geodetic Survey engineer. Under his able leadership the new organization continued to push technology to improve lighthouse efficiency. An example is the use of radio beacons which became an important element of navigation safety. The first one on the lakes was installed on the Lake Huron lightship in 1925.

The new commissioner had the authority to organize not more than 19 districts, each to be headed by a civilian inspector. An Army Corps of Engineer officer assigned to each district continued the role of providing professional expertise to lighthouse design, construction and maintenance. The entire organization was firmly under civilian control and leadership.

Growth was phenomenal. In 1852, there were 331 lighthouses and 42 lightships nationwide. By 1910, there were 1,462 lighthouses and 51 lightships! In 1925, the system reached a total of 1,951 lighthouses, 46 lightships and 14,900 other navigational aids.

As in the old U.S. Life-Saving Service, a viable retirement system was slow in coming. Keepers were forced to remain in their jobs, even if old or infirm since they had no other option. In 1916, for example, there were 92 keepers service-wide over 70 years old and 24 men with over 40 years of service. The life-savers finally got their retirement in 1915 when they merged with the U.S. Revenue-Marine to form the Coast Guard. Three years later Congress recognized the arduous nature of the Lighthouse Service work and authorized voluntary retirement at 65 after 30 years of service and mandatory retirement at 70.

On July 7, 1939, in another move for greater governmental efficiency, President Roosevelt abolished the Bureau of Lighthouses and transferred its duties to the Coast Guard. The Coast Guard operated under the Treasury Department, so lighthouses that had started under the Treasury Department had now returned.

As part of the process of integrating into the Coast Guard, lighthouse personnel were given the option of either retaining their civilian status or converting to a military position. About half of the keepers elected to transfer to a military position. The rest stayed as civilian keepers. The integration did not go smoothly. Many Lighthouse Service men had little desire to accept military discipline or customs. In fact, the Lighthouse Service had its own customs and traditions and were looking forward to celebrating its sesquicentennial on August 7, 1939, when FDR's unexpected mandate was issued. Roosevelt's action was a bitter blow to a proud service!

Construction

Most Great Lakes lighthouses were built during a relatively short period and are generally similar in construction. To withstand the ravages of storms, the lights were well constructed of brick or stone. Wood may have been used for mere range lights, but never for "real" lights. The structures tended to be square in shape and plain in design with no emphasis placed on anything "frivolous." The lights were not usually "one of a kind," but built from standard plans and designs. For example, the Au Sable Point

The Au Sable Point Lighthouse. Credit: Author's Collection

light, eight miles west of Grand Marais, Michigan, and the Outer Island light in the Apostle Islands, Wisconsin, were both built in 1874 from the same plans. Big Bay Point and Fourteen Mile Point lights, both on Lake Superior, were also near twins. In many instances however, the basic design was modified to meet a particular site requirement.

Usually the light station would consist of a compound of several buildings: the lighthouse proper, a combination tower and dwelling, an oil house and a fog signal house. A pier or dock was also built to facilitate the landing of personnel and supplies.

One of the problems of lighthouse construction significant to the Great Lakes was the terrible ice. While it usually had little effect on shore stations, for those on outlying reefs and shoals, it was a frightful problem. During the winter the lakes, especially the upper

The lighthouse at Spectacle Reef, Lake Huron. Credit: Author's Collection

lakes, freeze over. When the ice breaks up in the spring it often moves with the wind and current, crushing everything in its path, lighthouses included. Special precautions were needed both in building and design of the great offshore towers - for example at Stannard's Rock on Lake Superior and Spectacle Reef on Lake Huron - to enable them to standup to the power of the ice.

A number of lightships were also used on the lakes in the areas where vessel courses ran close to dangerous reefs or shoals, and it was impractical to erect a permanent lighthouse. In some instances, lightships were used until permanent stations were built.

Lamps, Lenses and Lights

The earliest lights on the Great Lakes used Argand lamps with parabolic reflectors. Argand lamps were developed by Aimee Argand of Geneva and used a burner with a hollow wick in a glass chimney. The first "standard" U. S. lamp was one known as a "Lewis" lamp. About 1812, Winslow Lewis convinced his good friend Stephen Pleasonton to buy a lamp he designed and patented based on those currently in use in Europe. This was all rather strange since Lewis once confessed he knew nothing about lighthouse optics! He called his device a "magnifying and reflecting lantern" for lighthouse work, which he claimed was a combined reflector, lamp and magnifier. Later experts called it ". . . as crude a device as ever emanated from the brain of an inventive man."[1] The reflectors were made of thin copper plate with a scanty silver coating. The lens, called a magnifier by Lewis, was a circular piece of green bottle glass two and a half by four inches in diameter. One inspector said it only, ". . . made a bad light worse." Another testified that it was ". . . worse than useless." Lewis did not argue against the criticism, but did point out the great savings in oil his device provided, using roughly half of that of the European lamps. He had also structured his contract such that instead of money, he was paid in oil, receiving one-half of the oil his device saved. After the first five years of his contract, his devices had saved so much oil

---

1 Frederick Talbot, Lightships and Lighthouses (Philadelphia: J.B. Lippincott Company, 1913), p. 34.

that the terms were modified by the government to one-third of the oil saved since the government believed it was too lucrative for Lewis! In its basic form the Lewis device used an Argand lamp inside of a parabolic reflector with the addition of a solid piece of glass as a crude lens. To increase the power of the light and its horizontal visibility, a number of lamps, each with its own reflector, were mounted together in a configuration called a chandelier. A series of rings, adjustment screws and other devices were used to hold the reflectors and lamps in the correct position. It was not uncommon to find 14 or more lamps in such an unwieldy arrangement. The light at Lake Huron's Bois Blanc Island for example, had 13 separate lamps, each with a fourteen inch reflector. The Lewis devices were complicated, inefficient and difficult to maintain. The parabolic reflectors were usually not well-made or true to form. After short use they were generally found to be bent and out of shape. The silvered

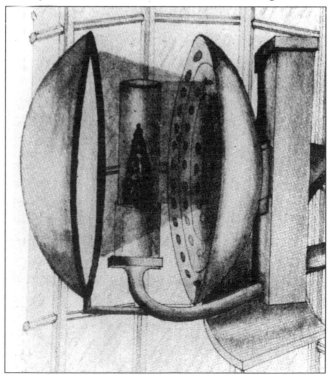

Argand lamp. Credit: U.S. Coast Guard

reflective surface in practice was scrubbed off in a matter of months because the issued cleanser was too abrasive. The lens itself attracted smoke, in turn dimming the light even more.

Between 1852—59, nearly all the Great Lakes lights were given the new Fresnel lens. The first Fresnel installed on the lakes was a fourth order at Waugoshance light on Lake Michigan. This lens has a powerful central lamp surrounded by refracting prisms and glass rings. The rings and prisms bend and guide the light, aiming it outward in powerful beams. In the old parabolic Lewis system, one-half of the light was lost. In the Fresnel system the loss was less than 10 percent, resulting in an increase of over 400 percent intensity! The Fresnel lenses were very heavy and were mounted on large steel pedestals. Weighing nearly three tons, a massive first order Fresnel lens had over 1,000 prisms. When it was necessary to revolve the light the lens was mounted on rollers or floated in a trough filled with mercury. They were so well balanced, a three-ton lens could be rotated by the touch of a finger! There are cases where through accident the mercury was lost and the keepers had to make a hurried trip to the local druggist to buy a replacement supply. Invented in 1820, the lens was named for Augustin Fresnel, a French scientist. Throughout its long use as a lighthouse appliance, the Fresnel lens was constantly improved in design and performance. Without question, it was the premier lighthouse lens ever developed.

Pleasonton was absolutely against the revolutionary lens and only tested it when forced to do so by Congress. Even when it proved wildly successful he refused their purchase. It was only with the removal of the infamous Fifth Auditor that the lens was accepted into service.

Fresnel lenses were classified into seven sizes or orders, relating to their power. A sixth order lens was less than a foot in diameter. The largest lens, a first order, measured six feet in diameter and stood nearly 12 feet high. The lenses were also very expensive, a factor that doubtless discouraged their early adoption by the penny-pinching Pleasonton. Eventually, the United States shifted

First order Fresnel lens. Credit: Author's Collection

Third order Fresnel lens from Au Sable Point, Lake Superior. Credit: Donald L. Nelson

to the Fresnel system and realized that as a result of their efficiency in reducing fuel costs, using only a quarter of previous requirements, they soon paid for themselves. The fuel savings resulted when only one lamp was needed for illumination as opposed to the many required by the Lewis system. Many of these wonderful lenses are now in museums where the public can view and appreciate the magnificent workmanship. Others were destroyed by vandals or official neglect when the lighthouses were abandoned by the government.

Great Lakes lights, as well as all others, burned sperm whale oil until about 1864. Two varieties were used, a thicker viscosity called "summer oil" and a thinner variant for winter use. In colder environments like Lake Superior, the oil had to be preheated before use to assure an even flow.

Today we tend to look on the use of whale oil as some sort of strange aberration from such a wondrous and majestic animal. "How could men kill such a magnificent creature just for something as mundane as oil?" What we forget is that it was whale oil that helped fuel the great industrial revolution, freeing families from slavery to the soil and allowing the galaxy of products that eventually gave us our technological society of today. On a very mundane basis, it was whale oil burning brightly and cleanly in a lonely little lighthouse that kept a ship off the deadly reef and saved all aboard. Sperm whale oil was used because simply stated, it was the best product available!

Having to warm the oil before use was often a problem, especially for a light located far out on the end of a long breakwater. The keeper had to carefully heat the oil ashore, then make his precarious way through storm and icy wind over a shaky wood walkway out to the light tower. Hopefully, by the time he arrived, the oil had not congealed too much for use. When the price of whale oil increased to a level the government thought too high, the fuel was switched initially to a lard oil and later to kerosene or, as it was then called, mineral oil.

The use of whale oil for lighthouses became a victim of the Civil War. The Confederate commerce raiders like the infamous *Shenandoah* and *Alabama* alone destroyed 46 New England whalers. Counting other loses, by the time the war ended fully half of the New England fleet was annihilated. As the result, whale oil prices dramatically increased.

Fresnel lens with kerosene burner. Credit: U.S. Coast Guard

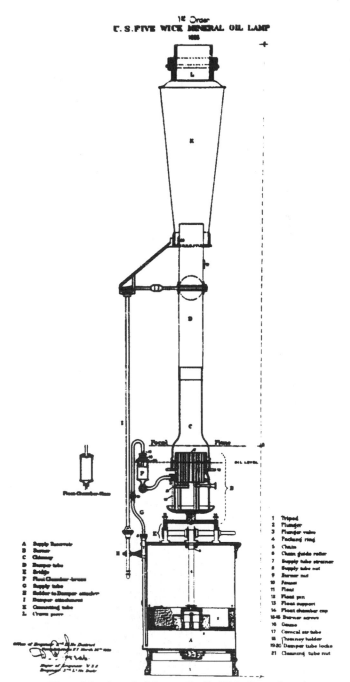

Five wick mineral oil lamp. Credit: U.S. Coast Guard

For a long time kerosene was thought to be too dangerous for lighthouse use. For example, in 1864, a Lake Michigan keeper used a kerosene lamp in his light without official approval to test its effectiveness. For several nights it apparently worked very well, its brilliance increasing the visibility of his light markedly. The next night it exploded, throwing burning oil on the keeper. A second explosion blew the lantern off the tower shattering the lens! Eventually the problems with the volatile fuel were solved and it proved highly successful. The fuel was burned through cylindrical lamp wicks, allowing for a central flow of air for improved and cleaner combustion. Arrangements of from one to five lamps were needed to provide the necessary candlepower for a given lens. By 1886, all lamps were converted to kerosene. The amount of kerosene burned was prodigious. For example, in 1916 over 600,000 gallons of kerosene were used in the country, more than half by the Lighthouse Service.

The ultimate improvement was made in 1904, when the service changed to the use of incandescent oil vapor lamps. Operating much like a Coleman lantern, fuel is forced into a vaporizer chamber and then into a mantle. This arrangement increased brilliance many times over the old-fashioned wicks. Today all lights are electric powered.

Oil, regardless of type, was a very carefully controlled item. It was easily pilferable as it could be burned in common lanterns, either by the keeper or sold by him to others. Today we could think of this in terms of having the keys to a government gas pump in your back yard. It could be very tempting to take just "a little" for use in the family car. Keepers were required to periodically measure the amount of oil used and record it in the logbook. Comparison with previous year records was another check for accountability. Inaccurate records, or tampering with them resulted in reprimand, suspension of pay or dismissal. Being bedridden with illness was not considered a reasonable excuse for not keeping proper records.

When acetylene was developed in the 1920s, it largely spelled the end for the old-time lightkeepers. The flow of gas for an acetylene lamp could be regulated by a "sun-valve" that would turn the light on and off as needed without human intervention. The first two lights equipped with this new technology were at St. Helena Island in northern Lake Michigan and Bois Blanc Island in Lake Huron just across the Straits of Mackinac in 1923 and 1924. No longer would the tower stairs echo to the tread of the old wickies' footfall at dusk and dawn.

Fog Signals

Fog signals were also maintained at many lights. At first they were only hand-rung bells, but by 1851 mechanically operated systems were in use. Later, steam whistles and sirens were adopted. By 1900, nearly all fog signals were of the steam powered variety. One problem with the steam whistle, however, was the long time needed to raise the necessary steam pressure before the signal could sound. Often the process of starting a boiler fire and waiting patiently for the steam pressure to rise to a sufficient level could take as long as 45 minutes. In a busy shipping channel this was a very long time indeed. Eventually steam signals were replaced with ones using compressed air that greatly decreased response time. The compressed air was provided by gasoline or diesel engines driving special air compressors and was stored in large tanks for instant use. Regardless of the type of signal, fog still could distort sound. In some instances, a fog signal can clearly be heard five miles from the station; lost at three miles and again heard at one mile.

Fog bell apparatus. Credit: U.S. Coast Guard

25

Early Lathrop hand-operated fog horn originally used at Au Sable Point light, Lake Superior. Credit: Donald L. Nelson

Steam fog whistle building of the type used at many Great Lakes stations. Credit: U.S. Coast Guard

*Fog whistle building at Poverty Island, Lake Michigan, circa 1913.
Credit: U.S. Coast Guard*

Flashing Lights

Developing a mechanism to make a light flash or occult, thus emitting a distinctive signal as opposed to a simple white glow, was a critical improvement to avoid confusion between lights. There were two general methods used; either to rotate the lamp and lens so that the beam was emitted only at preset intervals, or to rotate blinders around the lens. Power for either system came from a system of ropes or cables and weights wound to the top of the tower and allowed to slowly descend actuating a set of governing gears. Every so often, usually every three or four hours, the keepers had to crank the weight back up to begin the cycle again. In some instances, colored lights, flashing or constant, were used to differentiate lights.

Occulting clock, lens and lamp. Credit: U.S. Coast Guard

Canadian Lights

Lights on the Canadian side of the lakes were both similar and dissimilar to those in the United States. The Canadian lights initially suffered too from political patronage appointments instead of merit based. This wasn't unique to lighthouse keeping but was common throughout the public sector.

As in the United States, lighthouse construction followed the push westward. Starting in Lake Ontario, they moved into Lake Erie and then up Lake St. Clair to Lake Huron and Georgian Bay. In the beginning, Canadian lighthouses were operated by local commissions, using a variation of England's famous Trinity House. Canadian Trinity Houses, located at Montreal and Quebec, collected fees from vessels to support the lighthouses. When Upper Canada and Lower Canada were united in 1840, lighthouses came under the management of the Board of Works.

By mid-century it was evident that newer and improved navigation aids were needed to allow Canada to expand economically. Heavy lobbying by shipping interests and the Admiralty resulted in an enterprising three-year building program. Material and construction costs were to be paid by Britain, which made the plan all the better. For reasons not entirely clear, the resulting lighthouses are often called imperial towers. Six of the new lights were built on Lake Huron. Each tower was 80 feet tall, except for one 55-footer, and built of brick or masonry. This was in contrast to the more common Canadian practice of constructing wooden four or eight sided towers. Wood towers were cheap, using native lumber instead of expensive quarried rock and had the advantage of being easily moveable if erosion required relocation.

This Canadian lighthouse shows the typical four sided tower construction.
Credit Author's Collection

In the 1870s, the responsibility for lighthouses and other navigation aids passed from the Department of Works to the Department of Marine and Fisheries. There was no large support establishment as in the U.S.; no lighthouse board or other personnel other than a part-time engineer. The administration of lighthouses was accomplished by the Minister of Marine with his existing staff.

The United States may have had the first light on North America at Boston's Little Brewster Island in 1716, but Canada had the second, at Louisbourg on Cape Breton Island in 1734. Canada also has the distinction of having the oldest existing lighthouse on the Great Lakes. Gibraltar Point, at Toronto Island, was built in 1808, and decommissioned in 1907 after nearly a century of use. Canada also provided vital leadership in lighthouse technology. For example, Canadian lighthouse engineers developed mineral oil (kerosene) as a fuel well before the United States. In addition, the diaphone or compressed air foghorn was a 1902 invention of Toronto's J.P. Northery, Ltd.

Gibralter Point, Toronto. Credit: Author collection

As demand increased, in 1904 Canada bowed to the inevitable and formed a lighthouse board. Chaired by the Deputy Minister of Marine, it consisted of the chief engineer, commander of marine services, commissioner of lights and a shipping representative. It continued in existence until the 1930s, when its duties were turned over to the Department of Transport.

In one important regard, Canada trailed the United States, that of taking care of keepers and their families. In the United States, after the Lighthouse Board took over, a keeper and several assistants were common for every light. They also were usually well trained and had good quarters provided. Eventually, detailed instructions similar to those in use in the United States were written and promulgated by the Canadian authorities, but overall operations were always far "looser." In Canada, the keepers were usually alone with their families and left to their own devices. Lighthouse tenders customarily only visited twice a year to deliver fuel and other supplies, much less frequently than in the U.S. It was common for keepers and their families to remain at the loneliest of lights over the winter. The authorities did little to help them. In one instance, the keeper and his family at Cove Island in Georgian Bay nearly starved to death before the supply boat finally came at the end of the season.

Daily Routine

Running a light took a special kind of person. The daily routine could be difficult and was always demanding. It also was tedious and boring, depending on one's propensity for routine and repetitive work. The light had to be maintained in a constant state of readiness. The exact details of the keeper's responsibilities could be found in the publication *Instructions to Light-Keepers* provided by the Lighthouse Board. Virtually everything he needed to know was explained in laborious precision and detail. The main job of the keeper was to keep the lamp burning from sunset to sunrise. To this end, *Instructions* gave the keeper the daily responsibilities to clean and polish the lens, check and fill the oil lamp, dust the framework of the apparatus, trim the wicks and in general assure the light was ready in all regards for the next night. It is from the work of trimming the wick that the old keepers received the nickname, "wickies." Every two months he was to wash the lens with alcohol and once a year polish it with a special provided rouge. The lamps were changed every 15 days. The assistant keeper, if there was one, was tasked to clean the copper and brass fixtures of the apparatus and all tools in the lantern room as well as the walls, floors and balconies. He was to sweep the tower stairs, landing, doors, windows, recesses and passageways from the lantern to oil room. At some lights he also had to shovel the piles of dead birds off the galley deck every morning. Attracted by the bright beams, the birds were killed by the dozens when they crashed into the windows. Of course if there was no assistant at the light, the keeper had to do everything. When working in the lantern room, both men were required to wear linen aprons to prevent any chance of

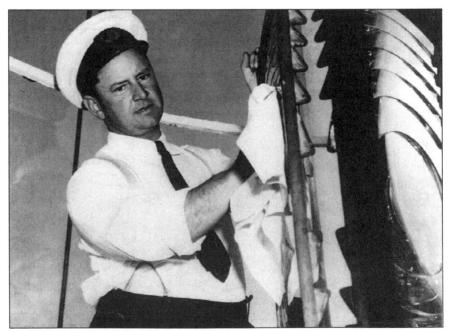

Cleaning the lens was part of the daily routine. Credit: U.S. Coast Guard

their coarse clothing scratching the valuable lens. Regulations called for the light to be ready for the night's use not later than 10:00 a.m. The grounds also had to be kept clean and orderly as well as all buildings and facilities. Station maintenance, including painting the tower, consumed the bulk of the men's time. Female keepers were excused from having to paint the tower.

Lights on the Great Lakes were not exhibited year around. Usually they were closed sometime in December and not reopened until mid-March or later. The exact dates depended on the opening and closing of shipping. In some locations on Lake Michigan they were kept burning all year, but this is an anomaly.

Before *Instructions* any training the keeper received was at best haphazard. The superintendent (in reality the collector of customs) was supposed to instruct the new keeper in his duties, but this was not always done and was usually very rudimentary at best. If the new keeper was very lucky, the old one gave him detailed instructions before leaving. Usually this didn't happen. There was a written sent of instructions that was supposed to be posted at each light, but the 1851 investigation discovered more of the stations without it than with it. This lack of adequate training and reference instructions can partially explain the disastrous condition of the lights before the era of the Lighthouse Board.

To help provide fresh vegetables, keepers often kept small gardens. In many instances they were not very successful since the lights were usually located in areas that did not have good soil. In some instances keepers brought boxes of their own garden soil with them. For many years this was the practice of the keeper at Stannard's Rock Light. Located 44 miles out in Lake Superior, almost directly north of Marquette, Michigan, the light is often lashed by thundering storms. As a result the keeper constantly "lost" his gardens to the grasping waves. Raising chickens was also popular at many lighthouses, but there could be problems. At one station the foghorn blew so loudly the chickens refused to lay eggs.

At another a big wind came and just blew the chickens away, coop and all. At least the cow stayed on the ground!

The Lighthouse Service also provided special portable libraries. Packed into sets of roughly 50 books, the library boxes could easily be exchanged between stations. As an added bonus, the boxes were designed to stack into neat bookshelves, thus helping to minimize furniture requirements. Other keepers occupied their spare time building model boats, hunting, fishing, canning, taxidermy, agate picking or mulling through correspondence courses.

The tenders often worked in terrible weather conditions. In this photo the Crocus *is covered with thick Lake Erie ice. Credit: U.S. Coast Guard*

The lights were supplied by special vessels called lighthouse tenders. The first government owned tender on the lakes was the schooner *Belle*, purchased in 1863, for use in the Eleventh District. Previously the work was done by contract vessels. Other famous tenders used at various times were *Dahlia, Haze, Crocus, Hyacinth, Warrington, Marigold, Lotus, Amaranth, Clover* and *Aspen*. These tough little vessels carried not only all the operating stores needed by the lights, but also the dreaded inspector. These men were infamous for their, "white glove" examinations of stations. A poor inspection report could spell the end of a keeper's career.

The tender Amarnath *carefully comes alongside the Detour Reef station.*
Credit: U.S. Coast Guard

Before the advent of the Lighthouse Board and its system of depots and tenders, the entire chain of lighthouses were virtually administered, at least in the field, by contract. Pleasonton issued a series of five-year contracts for all supplies needed by the whole Service, as well as complete maintenance of all apparatus. The contractor was to visit each light once a year and provide Pleasonton with a written report of its condition and an evaluation of the ability of the keeper. Subletting was common, further denigrating the effective execution of the requirements.

Some men handled the deadly daily routine of lightkeeping well. Others however, after a careful reading of their daily logs, appeared to "lose their marbles." More than one keeper was driven over the edge of sanity by the terrible grinding isolation and lack of human contact.

Educating the keeper's children was frequently a problem. If possible, the Service tried to station the keeper near enough to a school but many times this wasn't possible. However, it is apparent the Service expended every effort to transfer keepers with families to lights near schools. A frequent solution when schools were not available was to board the children with a family in town. Such expenses of course were paid by the keeper, not the government.

Keepers also maintained careful logbooks of the weather, vessels passing the station and other items of daily activity. Inspectors admonished the keepers if they became too flowery or personal in their entries. After all, it was an official government journal, not a diary!

A lighthouse was often a family enterprise where the husband and wife teamed up to make the light a success. The husband as keeper assumed full responsibility for the light proper, while the wife took charge of the dwelling. The children pitched in where they could too. Everyone worked to "keep the light."

The feared inspector was supposed to arrive unannounced, but the Service version of the "jungle telegraph" usually gave the keepers adequate warning. When telephones were finally installed at the isolated stations a friendly call from someone at headquarters generally gave fair warning that the inspector was on his way. When a Lake Michigan inspector tried driving to some of the closer stations by car, friends of the keepers also gave warning. When the inspector left the main highway and turned down the gravel road to the station, someone with a telephone inevitably spotted him and called the local keeper giving him enough time for a final brush-up. If he was arriving by tender and the day was foggy, the distinctive sound of the vessel's engines gave away its presence. In clear weather the inspector's pendant was visible on the mast.

Once the inspector was spotted, the station crew went into a flurry of activity. Last minute dusting and cleaning, straightening up and polishing were the order of the hour. Children hurried to put away toys and help where ever possible. The keeper donned his best uniform and family their Sunday finest. If the inspector had a weakness for hot apple pie or other baked goods, the wife tried to whip up a fresh batch.

Lighthouse inspectors often used this husband-wife team effort to their advantage. After carefully examining the husband's light, he would pull the man aside and say something to the effect that he was doing a fine job but that his wife was letting him down. She just wasn't keeping the quarters up to standard. Perhaps the keeper could encourage her to do a better job. When he finished checking the quarters, the inspector would pull the wife aside and tell her the same thing about the husband's performance; the house looked great but the light wasn't up to snuff! Such a management method doubtless led to interesting family discussion as the inspector's gig pulled away from the dock.

In the early days, keepers often moonlighted with other jobs as a way of making up for the poor pay. Fishing, farming and lumbering were popular sidelines to their official duties. As the Service matured, such practices were usually forbidden.

In the 1880s, Nathaniel Fadden, the keeper at Lake Superior's Manitou Island, Michigan, reportedly operated a still at the lighthouse that produced an especially powerful strain of rotgut whiskey. Producing booze at the light was bad enough, but he apparently also sold it to the local Indians. Since Manitou Island, just off the tip of the Keweenaw Peninsula, was about as remote as you can get, his activities were not easily noticed. Things got out of hand in 1886 when arguments over price and quality resulted in a farcical Indian attack on the light. When the situation was finally understood by the authorities, Fadden was dismissed and jailed.

Lightkeeping was a job constantly in transition. From the freewheeling days of the Fifth Auditor to the tight control of the Coast Guard, requirements, procedures and technology continued to evolve. The tales of the men and women who kept the lights now are only remembered in the old logbooks, yellowed news clippings and fading memories of the few old-time keepers still left. The colorful and exciting era of Great Lakes lighthouses is dead but hopefully not yet forgotten.

References

Adamson, Hans Christian, *Keepers of the Lights* (New York: Greenberg, 1955), pp. 319-335.

Annual Report of the Lighthouse Board (Washington, DC: US Department of the Treasury, various issues).

Appleton, Thomas, *Usque ad Mare, A History of Canadian Coast and Marine Services* (Ottawa: Department of Transportation, 1968), pp. 105-111.

"A Brief History of Canadian Lighthouses," [*http://members.aol.com/* stiffcrust/pharos/index.html#imperial]. November 5, 1997.

"Canada's Georgian Bay," [*http://www.biddeford.com/lhdigest/* sept96/georgia.html]. October 28, 1997.

Capron, Captain Walter C., *The U.S. Coast Guard* (New York: Franklin Watts, Inc., 1965), pp. 121-127.

Van Hoey, Mike, "Lights of the Straits," *Michigan History Magazine*, September/October, 1986, pp. 24-25.

Holland, Francis Ross, Jr., *America's Lighthouses, An Illustrated History* (New York: Dover Publications, 1988), pp. 1-54.

Instructions to Light-Keepers (Allen Park: Michigan: Great Lakes Lighthouse Keepers Association, 1989).

Barry James and Grant Day, *History and Archaeology of the First Copper Harbor Lighthouse*, Report of Investigations Number 21 (Archaeology Laboratory, Department of Social Sciences, Michigan Technological University, Houghton Michigan, 1995), pp. 5-32; 99.

Johnson, Arnold B., *The Modern Lighthouse Service* (Washington, DC: 1890), pp. 17-19.

Johnson, Robert Erwin, *Guardians of the Sea, History of the United States Coast Guard, 1915 to the Present* (Annapolis, Maryland: Naval Institute Press, 1987), pp. 161-163.

National Maritime Initiative, *1994 Inventory of Historic Light Stations* (Washington, DC: US Department of the Interior, National Park Service, 1994).

Donald L. Nelson, correspondence with author, March 9, 1996.

Putnam, George R., *Lighthouses and Lightships of the United States* (New York: Houghton Mifflin Company, 1917), pp. 185-193; 196; 203; 231-232; 237-239.

Wayne Sapulski, "The Imperial Towers," *Great Lakes Cruiser*, pp. 25-29.

Talbot, Frederick A., Lightships and Lighthouses (Philadelphia: J.B. Lippincott Company, 1913), pp. 29-31; 33-37;42-48; 209-210.

U.S. Department of Commerce, Lighthouse Service, *The United States Lighthouse Service, 1915* (Washington, DC: Government Printing Office, 1916), pp. 32-37; 40-56; 60-64; 73-77; 81-83.

Weiss, George, *The Lighthouse Service, its History, Activities and Organization* (Baltimore: The Johns Hopkins Press, 1916), pp. 4-10.

Whipple, A.B.C., *The Whalers* (Alexandria, Virginia: Time-Life Books, 1979), pp. 155-157.

Chapter Two

Death at Oswego Light

Sometimes simple things turn terribly tragic. A perfect plan just crumbles and the result is disastrous. An example happened at Oswego, New York on December 4, 1942.

Old-timers at Oswego remembered it as the worst gale in 30 years. Not since the infamous 1913 freshwater hurricane tore through Lake Ontario was Oswego pummeled by a storm of such intense ferocity. Powerful winds of 65 mph blew steady, tearing out trees and knocking down electric power and telephone lines. House-sized waves smashed into the harbor, tossing rocks weighing several tons around like a child's wooden blocks. One massive five-ton boulder was rolled up and over the breakwater! Snow drifted heavy across the landscape further adding to the feeling of desolation.

Far out in the Oswego West Pierhead Light the keeper, Boatswain's Mate First Class Karl A. Jackson, waited with increasing impatience. The rage of the storm had marooned him in the isolated tower for the last three days and he was ready to leave his lonely prison. Five times he blew signals with the foghorn asking for relief. Where were they? Rations were getting short and he was just plain hungry! When would they come?

The Oswego breakwater light, circa 1945. Credit: U.S. Coast Guard

The breakwater light, built in 1930, sits on top of a square concrete foundation. It is about 10 feet from the water to the top of the landing deck. A steel ladder set in the concrete provided access from the water. The structure perches at the end of the west breakwater, about a half mile off shore.

Just past 10:00 a.m., the 38-foot wood picket boat left the Oswego Coast Guard Station at East Cove and headed for the light. The small boat drove on through the cresting gray waves, shouldering them aside as it continued to work its way deliberately to the light. Aboard were two relief keepers, Bert E. Egelston and Carl Sprague and eight other Coast Guardsmen. The extra men were needed to help fend off the boat when it lay alongside the concrete foundation of the light to transfer the keepers. Although the boat would be under the lee of the breakwater and sheltered from the worst of the storm, additional help was needed. Lt. (jg) Alston J. Wilson, 54, the commanding officer of the station and captain of the port, a 35-year Coast Guard veteran, was in command of the vessel. By the time the boat left the station the storm had moderated, with the wind down to 30 mph and the waves somewhat diminished, but it was still very rough. Although the conditions were bad, Wilson believed the transfer could be safely made.

A Coast Guard 38-foot picket boat similar to the one at Oswego.
Credit: Donald L. Nelson

He was right. The transfer was made successfully. Wilson carefully brought the picket boat up to the ladder, the extra crew fended it off and both keepers scampered up the steel rungs to safety. Timing his move gingerly, Jackson dropped down the ladder and jumped into the tossing boat without injury. To this point it was a job well done.

The boat backed away from the concrete foundation of the light easily, but when the gasoline engine was shifted into forward, it inexplicably quit. The boat immediately started drifting fast west to east right across the harbor mouth and began a violent motion, caused by the enormous waves and powerful current from the Oswego River. Twice the engineer, Machinist's Mate First Class Fred Ruff, in the small engine room was able to start the stalled engine. Each time the balky engine quickly coughed to a stop.

Lt. Wilson then ordered the 125-pound anchor dropped to check the boats' drift. Second Class Seaman Irving Ginsburg and Second Class Bos'ns Mate Eugene C. Sisson crawled out on the iced-up and violently pitching bow and released it.

The anchor immediately dug deep into the soft bottom of the harbor. The bow of the picket boat swung into the wind and the progress toward disaster was checked. Now there was time to either get the engine going or for a rescue boat to come out from the station and tow them back to the dock. Then the inch-and-a-half manila anchor line snapped. In the powerful wind and waves it had held for a bare ninety seconds.

At the outer end of the east breakwater was a small beacon known as East Light. It is protected by a rock barrier. Now the boat began a fight between wind and current. If the wind won, the boat would hit the east breakwater at a point where there was some protection from the west breakwater since it was partially under its lee. Although the boat would be lost, the men would likely be safe. If the current was proven the stronger, the boat would probably end up in calmer water, allowing time for either repair or rescue. The combination of the two forces, however, kept the boat trapped in a deadly course for the sharp-edged rocks surrounding East Light.

The testimony of Chief Boatswain's Mate John Mixon, the second in command of the station, and First Class Machinist's Mate Fred L. Ruff, the only survivors, can recreate the last moments of the boat. Lt. Wilson was in the small pilothouse with Ginsburg, Sisson and Mixon. Ginsburg and Sisson soon went on deck, apparently uncomfortable in the small, closed-in cabin. Before Wilson followed them up, he turned the wheel over to Mixon. Adrift or not, the wheel must be manned. Jackson, First Class Seaman Leslie J. Holdsworth, and Second Class Machinist's Mate Ralph J. Sprau were on deck in the aft cockpit. Ruff was in the engine room desperately still trying to get the engine working. Mixon remembered Wilson as utterly calm, giving orders as if he were back in the office. Disaster may be imminent, but he kept his wits clear!

The boat was being driven rapidly eastward, parallel to the breakwater. The bow was pointing toward the distant shore. The Coast Guardsmen would be all right, if they only would clear the end of the rocks. It was not to be!

A large wave surged under the boat and sped it towards the murderous rocks. Realizing what was happening, Wilson yelled, "Look out, she's hitting."

The boat crashed on the port side with tremendous force, the impact shattering her planking and rolling her over, dumping the men on deck into the frigid water. The backwash swung the boat out to sea, with the bow pointing into the lake. As the boat righted itself, another wave again smashed it into the rocks, tearing a hole ten-foot long and three-foot wide into the starboard side. The overturned boat then drifted off into the stormy lake.

Mixon was trapped inside the pilothouse and only escaped by smashing out a window and diving through into the water. When he finally surfaced, he was being carried along by the current but was able to grasp a jagged rock at the end of the breakwater. With a strength born only of desperation, he somehow was able to climb the slippery rocks of the ten-foot high breakwater to safety. He did not remember how he accomplished it!

Ruff recalled that when the boat first rolled, the engine room flooded with three feet of water let in through a ventilator hatch. After it righted and hit again, he scrambled out through the hatch to the deck. Finding himself 10 feet from the end of the light, he quickly considered the situation then jumped for it. After a short swim he also reached safety on the breakwater.

From his precarious perch on the ice covered breakwater Mixon looked for his shipmates. Other than Ruff, he saw five of the six men left struggling in the rough water. Sisson was about 60 feet out battling in the boiling waves. Sprau was 200 feet away, desperately trying to swim to the breakwater. Both were caught in the current and being rapidly carried out into the lake.

Wilson and Ginsburg were swimming in the lee of the east breakwater. All the men were struggling to reach the safety of the rocks. Jackson was holding on to the broken anchor line that was still fast to the picket boat. The boat itself was barely awash and drifting 300-400 feet to the east.

Wilson's oilskins had trapped an air pocket, which was helping the officer to stay afloat. When a big wave pushed him closer to the breakwater, Mixon although exhausted and shaking uncontrollably from the cold, scrambled down the rocks with the intention of diving in to help him. When Wilson saw what Mixon was going to do, he calmly told him, "Don't try it. Save your own life John." Wilson then stopped struggling. He had issued his last command.

Ginsburg continued to fight to reach the rocks. For a while he swam overhand. Then he tried side stroke and later on his back. Unable to beat the powerful current, he finally sank forever beneath the cold waves.

Jackson soon loosened his death grip on the anchor line, dropped off and sank too. Some observers on shore thought he may have managed to climb on the bow, only later to slip off into the lake. In the blowing scud and snow they could not be certain just what they saw.

Mixon and Ruff slowly began to work their way from the outer end of the 2,100 foot breakwater toward shore. The breakwater did not extend all the way to the beach. There was a gap of 250 feet between it and land. For a while they crawled painfully on hands and knees to keep from being swept into the lake. Countless times they slipped on the icy rocks and fell. Each time they got back up and fought onward toward the shore.

When they saw the picket boat was in trouble, the men at the station sounded the alarm and desperately worked to get a rescue boat underway. Second Class Boatswain's Mate Robert Burnet, left in charge of the station, bellowed, "Get the 36 boat going, now!" The big 36-foot motor lifeboat was on its cradle in the boathouse and had already been laidup for the winter. But their shipmates were in danger and with unheard of speed, it was oiled, fueled, serviced and run down the rails into the water. It took a bare 18 minutes to get going at full throttle, bashing its way through the seas to the rescue. Burnet was at the helm. Six other Coast Guardsmen stood ready for action in the cockpit.

Afraid to try to lay the motor lifeboat directly against the rocks of the breakwater to rescue Mixon and Ruff, Burnet sent two men, Coxswains Sanford Gregory and John F. Black over in a small skiff trailing a line back to the lifeboat. By this time Mixon and Ruff had made it about 1,600 feet down the breakwater. The hope was to get both men into the skiff, then haul it to the big boat with the line. However in the fury of the gale, the skiff smashed against the rocks, stranding both rescuers with the victims and losing the line in the process.

Deciding Ruff and Mixon and his two men were in less immediate danger than those farther out, Burnet pulled away and headed out for the awash picket boat. When they found Wilson's body still floating, he asked for a volunteer to try to recover it. Second Class Seaman Andrew W. Cisternino volunteered, tied a rope to his waist and dove into the furious 40 degree water.

He reached the body and grabbed it tightly but as he was being hauled back to the boat, the cold numbed his arms and unable to control them, the body slipped away in the waves. Only with the greatest difficulty was the boat crew, numbed with cold and balancing precariously on the icy deck, able to drag Cisternino back aboard. Wrapped in heavy blankets he was hustled below. When the boat eventually returned to the dock, he was immediately hospitalized for exposure.

To those on shore, the rescue effort was especially dramatic. The motor lifeboat repeatedly disappeared in the trough between the huge seas, giving the impression that it too had sunk. Each time it reappeared to continue on with its work.

Anxious family members waited at the Coast Guard dock for the motor lifeboat to return. Some hoped their men on the ill-fated picket boat had somehow been saved from an icy death. Others prayed for the safe return of the motor lifeboat crew.

With no other choice open to him, Burnet decided he had to risk the boat to rescue the four men on the breakwater. He knew that a mistake on his part could not only wreck the boat but put his crew into the same circumstance that the picket boat men ended up in. Using every ounce of skill and experience, Burnet brought the big boat right up to the rocks and neatly picked off the stranded men. It was a masterful piece of seamanship! The four bedraggled men were taken below to join Cisternio and Burnet headed for the dock.

Ruff, Mixon and Gregory were immediately hospitalized. In a classic case of understatement concerning Burnet's work in rescuing them, Mixon said, "Bob did a fine job."

The broken, battered picket boat soon washed ashore and Coast Guardsmen waded out waist deep into the cold surf to search it for the bodies of their shipmates. None were found. For several days following the disaster, Coast Guardsmen and soldiers from nearby Fort Ontario patrolled the wind-swept beaches looking for bodies. Their efforts were fruitless.

History has a way of repeating itself. An old-timer remembered that during the 1913 gale lighthouse keeper Dan Sullivan was marooned at the west light for a full week. Part of the time he, too, was without food. After signaling his wife of his predicament, she told a friend who managed to fight his way out through the tumultuous lake with provisions.

A similar incident occurred on Saturday, December 20, 1851. During a terrific wind and snow storm, old Captain Samuel Freeman, the Oswego lightkeeper, obtained a small boat and with the help of two friends, rowed out to the light to assure it was ready for the coming night. He knew several ships were due that night and without its steady glow disaster was imminent. The vessels would be looking for a light that wasn't there! Catastrophe struck when Captain Freeman and his men were returning to shore. Unable to manage the boat in the crashing waves, it drifted into the surf where it capsized. The three men hung desperately to the overturned hull. Captain Malcolm Bronson had watched Freeman's progress closely from an east side dock. When he saw the accident and that death was sure to grab the men, he found three volunteers to help him launch a small boat into the tumultuous seas. After a desperate fight against both waves and ice, he and his men reached them and hauled them aboard their boat. They reached the water-logged men just in the nick of time as death was very close to claiming them. A few more minutes and they would have been gone. All reached safety in a near-frozen condition. Freeman was speechless and senseless and for some time it was thought death would still take the brave old lightkeeper. In the end he survived. Both boat crews displayed magnificent courage, as did the crews in 1942. In 1851 and 1913, it was tragedy averted. In 1942, it was death at Oswego Lighthouse.

The tragedy and heroism of that terrible day was ignored for over half a century. Happening when it did, in the midst of World War II, other events captured the public's imagination. On December 4, 1996, fifty-four years to the day, the Coast Guard and city of Oswego formally memorialized the event. Survivors of the accident, family members and representatives of the city boarded the station's 44-foot motor lifeboat and motored to the vicinity of the disaster, placing a memorial wreath in the icy waters of Lake Ontario. The solemn ceremony occurred at 10:25 a.m., exactly the time of the 1942 accident. The city also plans to erect more permanent memorials, one near the lighthouse and the other in Veteran's Park. One of the participants was David Ginsburg, the father of Irving Ginsburg, killed in the wreck. Now 98 years old, he vowed never to return to Oswego until some kind of memorial was established. It took a long time, but finally the brave men received the recognition so richly deserved.

References

Inland Seas (Spring 1997), p. 50.

Penrose, Laurie, *A Traveler's Guide to 100 Eastern Great Lakes Lighthouses* (Davison, Michigan: Freide Publications, 1994), p.48.

————. "Memorial For Six Coast Guardsmen Lost in 1942 is Long Overdue," *On Scene* (Spring, 1997), p. 7.

————. *Oswego Daily Times* (Oswego, New York), December 23, 1851;

————. *Palladium-Times* (Oswego, New York), December 3, 4, 5, 7, 8, 9, 10, 1942.

Townsend, Robert B., ed., *Tales From the Great Lakes* (Toronto, Ontario: Dundurn Press, 1995), pp. 152-153

Chapter 3

"Let the Lower Lights be Burning"

*L*ighthouses have long penetrated the popular culture, especially during the 19th Century when maritime commerce was so
much more important to people than it is today. The tall lighthouse
tower stood squarely for faithfulness and eternal vigilance against
an ever-grasping sea. Mariners, sail or steam, depended on its
steady beam to guide them to safety on dark and storm swept seas
or lakes. There was almost an emotional relationship to the lighthouse and its steadfast beacon.

Lighthouses have even become part of gospel music. The most
famous example is *"Let the Lower Lights be Burning,"* written in 1871
by Philip Paul Bliss. The sea and sailing were popular themes for
hymns during this period. Another example is *"Jesus, Savior, Pilot
Me,"* written in 1871 by Edward Hopper, an American Presbyterian
minister. All the various hymns spoke in terms sailors understood,
charts, waves, treacherous rocks, compasses and the absolute need
for a competent pilot to guide them. The origins of *"Lower Lights"*
are somewhat murky, or at best there are a number of variations.
The most popular version of how the song came to be, as quoted
from the *Memoir of Philip D. Bliss* is that "On a dark and stormy
night when the waves rolled like mountains and not a star was to
be seen, a boat rocking and plunging neared the Cleveland harbor.
'Are you sure this is Cleveland?' asked the captain seeing only one
light from the lighthouse. 'Quite sure, sir' replied the pilot. 'Where

are the lower lights?' 'Gone out, sir!' 'Can you make the harbor?' 'We must or perish, sir!' And with a strong hand and a brave heart the old pilot turned the wheel. But, alas, in the darkness he missed the channel, and with a crash up the rocks, the boat was shivered, and many a life lost in a watery grave. Brethren, the Master will take care of the Great Lighthouse: let us keep the lower lights burning!"

At the time Cleveland was marked by a lighthouse high on the hill that served well in showing mariners far out on the lake where the city was, but did little for helping them past the rock breakwater and into the harbor. A smaller light on the end of the breakwater served this purpose. With the small light out, getting into the harbor was guesswork.

The story goes that the Reverend Dwight L. Moody used the story as a sermon at his Chicago tabernacle following the disaster. Inspired by Moody's eloquence, Bliss put the tale into the form of a hymn, the words of which run:

Brightly beams our Father's Mercy
From His Lighthouse ever more;
But to us he gives the keeping
Of the Lights along the shore.

Chorus
Let the lower lights be burning
Send a gleam across the waves;
Some poor, fainting, struggling seaman
You may rescue, you may save.

Dark the night of sin has settled
Loud the angry billows roar;
Eager eyes are watching, longing
For the lights along the shore.

Trim your feeble lamp, my brother
Some poor sailor, tempest-tost
Trying now to make the harbor
In the darkness, may be lost.

The hymn became extremely popular, not only with Great Lakes sailors, but also with mariners all over the world. It was reportedly a favorite of lightkeeper Knudsen whose story appears in the "Jump for it" chapter. It was also a special favorite of Captain Bundy, who sailed his gospel ship *Glad Tidings* and its successors around the lakes in the 1880s and 1890s. Whenever he arrived in port he did his best to convert the sailors from their traditional ne'er-do-well ways, usually without much success. "Lower Lights" was an important part of his musical arsenal. Although Cleveland is the usual setting for the story, some people believe it was Avon Point, near Cleveland or even Buffalo, New York.

References

Association for Great Lakes Marine History, Newsletter (May 1993), p. 3.

Bowen, Dana Thomas, *Memories of the Lakes* (Cleveland, Ohio: Freshwater Press, 1969), pp. 160-165.

De Wire, Elinor, *Guardians of the Lights: The Men and Women of the U.S. Lighthouse Service* (Sarasota, Florida: Pineapple Press, 1995), pp. 130-131.

Larsen, Dorathea F., correspondence with author, April 20; May 6, 1994.

Ivan Walton Collection, Bentley Historical Library, University of Michigan, box 4.

Whittle, D. W., ed., *Memoir of P. P. Bliss.* p. 114.

Where is No. 82?

Lightships are tough little boats built to stay on station in the worst weather, to keep their beacon lit and horn blowing. Regardless of storm conditions they were never to leave station without orders. As the result of this single-minded tenacity to say at their post, disaster sometimes stuck. The tale of lightship *No. 82* is a case in point.

The old Buffalo lightship, shown here with "86" on her bow. Note the daymark on her foremast, fog bell forward and turtleneck bow. Credit: U.S. Coast Guard

No. 82 was built in 1912, at the Muskegon, Michigan, yard of the Racine-Truscott-Shell Lake Boat Company. Her strong steel hull had a whaleback forecastle deck, a single lantern mast forward and a small fore and aft rigged jigger mast on the stern. The stern mast could help steady her on station during a breeze. The smokestack stood roughly amidships. Length overall was 95 feet and beam 21 feet. A single 90 horsepower coal-fired engine gave her some small degree of maneuverability. In theory it was enough to move on and off station but in practice the vessels were usually towed by a tender or tug.

The classic lightship was high in the bow and of heavy overall construction. She was built to stay in position and to kill if required. There is always the danger of collision. Should such a calamity happen, it is the lightship that will survive. The loss of the merchant vessel is bad enough, but the loss of the lightship provided the chance of other ships to blunder into the reef without the lightship there to warn them away. It is better to have one ship wrecked than many. Therefore, make the lightship strong! There were 150 instances nationwide of major collisions between lightships and other vessels. Only five resulted in the loss of the lightship, not a bad average speaking highly of the construction of the tough little ships.

The number of lightships in service peaked in 1909, when 56 were employed in all American waters. On the Great Lakes, 20 different lightships saw service at 18 different locations between 1891 - 1970.

Because of the desolation of lightship duty, efforts were made to make them comfortable. The captain and mate had their quarters aft. Crew quarters were on the berth deck, with bunks sloping to prevent the men from rolling out during violent motion. The standard lighthouse library chest was provided to help while away the long hours of boredom. Sea chests provided storage for personal gear and doubled as seats. A small, well-equipped galley with mess tables was available for meals. Different methods were used to keep china on the table during rough weather. Wet tablecloths and edging both had their adherents. On some lightships it was popular to drill holes in the table top in which small pegs were fitted, erecting a little fence around each dish, bowl or cup. Regardless of such precautions, on a truly "lively" day, nothing could keep the dish on the table. The food was common to sailors everywhere, even to include

Meal time on a lightship. Credit: Author's Collection

"scouse," an amorphous combination of salt beef, potatoes and onions, with other items as the galley might have surplus.

The daily routine on the lightship was common throughout the service. The work day began when the lantern was lowered at sunrise. At 6:20 a.m., the captain or mate called the crew with a loud, "All hands," yelled into the berthing deck. At 7:30 a.m., the lamps were taken below and carefully cleaned. When the weather was

Cleaning the lens. Credit: Author's Collection

calm the job took only a couple of hours. When the seas were kicking up, the time could easily double. Once this job was done, little remained to be done other than normal watch-keeping and cleaning ship. At sundown the lamps went back up the masts. Typically the mate took one watch and the captain the other.

The illuminating apparatus on *No. 82* consisted of a cluster of three 300 mm oil lens lanterns on a sleeve hoisted to the masthead. The fog signal was provided by a ten-inch steam whistle. A hand operated bell provided backup.

Fog was always dreaded, not only because of the inherent visibility problems and increased chance of collision, but also it meant the whistle or bell had to be sounded. Its mournful blast added immeasurably to the general feeling of depression for the crew. The longer the fog lasted, the worse it became.

Lightkeeping on a lightship was far worse than that ashore or on a tower station. Ashore a man had the opportunity to take a walk, maybe visit a friend or receive company. Isolation was not normally an appalling problem. On the fixed tower such as Stannard's Rock, Lake Superior, long walks were out of the question and isolation was a constant companion. But at least on either a shore station of fixed tower the damn things didn't move. A man could plant his feet firmly on rock or ground and not be forced to hold on for dear life! The lightships, however, were rarely still, whether the weather was fair or foul. The most experienced sailors often suffered awful bouts of seasickness from the unique motion of their ships. The peculiar pitching and rolling motion made even cast-iron stomachs squeamish. One saltwater man remarked, "If it weren't for the disgrace it would bring to my family, I'd rather go to the state's prison."[2]

Even in calm weather the motion on a lightship was different than a normal vessel underway. For a couple of minutes she will lay steady, then suddenly roll the scuppers under. One captain there

2 Gustav Kobbe, *Life on the South Shoal Lightship.*

always said they, "Washed own decks." For this reason hull ports were rarely opened. Kept on a short scope of anchor, the ship was unable to respond normally to the might of the sea, forcing her to butt into the waves, sending heavy deluges of water rolling down the open decks.

During the fall and spring, the tough little ships took a beating, not only from storm stress, but also from ice. Spray quickly froze on the masts and cabins, thickly covering her in a translucent coating. The crews spent many wearying hours with axes smashing ice clear of hatches and other critical areas.

Lightship *No. 82* was delivered to the Lighthouse Service on July 12, 1912, and on August 3, was placed on station, 13 miles off the entrance to Buffalo harbor, Lake Erie. Four, four-ton mushroom anchors fore and aft with heavy chain secured to her keelson, held her firmly in position.

Many historians believe the great storm of 1913 was the most devastating ever to strike the Great Lakes. By the time it finally blew itself out, 19 vessels were totally destroyed, another 52 damaged and approximately 250 sailors dead. Fifteen big steel vessels were lost; 11 just disappeared with all hands. Its colossal ferocity caused it often to be referred to as a freshwater hurricane.

The tremendous storm was actually the result of the combination of two separate weather systems. The Great Lakes weather stations had been carefully watching an approaching high pressure system rolling down from the northwest. Its rotation was clockwise. A large low pressure system moving across the southern U.S. from west to east was discounted. It clearly was too distant to influence the Great Lakes. It was a counterclockwise system. As this second system approached the Atlantic, it suddenly and unexpectedly veered first north, then to the northwest. Both collided brutally over the Great Lakes and there was hell to pay.

Not only did the forecasters fail to appreciate the power of the colliding systems, but experienced captains did, too! Worse, they even ignored the storm warnings posted at lake ports on November 7. What was one more fall storm? "We gutted out many before, so what is one more blow?"

The storm blew for four terrible days. On Lake Huron and Erie the winds started in the northwest, then went northeast, then north and finally back to northwest. Where the wind gages even stayed up speeds were recorded as exceeding 90 miles per hour. On the open lake true speed measurements were almost impossible to record. In a lake as shallow as Erie the waves piled up into house-size mountains of churning water.

The south shore of Lake Erie was battered badly. Eight-feet-high snowbanks blocked roads, downed telephone and power lines littered the landscape. Road and rail traffic stopped solid. Communication, both road movement and electrical, ceased due to the weather attack.

Aboard *No. 82* was a crew of six men. Hugh M. Williams was the captain and Andrew Leahy, mate; Charles W. Butler, chief engineer; Cornelius Leahy, assistant engineer and mate's brother, and Peter Mackey and William Jensen, crewmen.

What exactly happened on the lightship will of course never be known. But when the full force of the storm struck it must have been hell on the small ship. Held on her short anchor scope, the ship shouldered her way into the growing northwest seas. Built into monsters by the powerful blasts of wind, comber after comber broke over the stubby bow and rolled down the deck, sweeping all loose gear before their white foaming crests. The water that flooded through any minor gaps in hatch seals was managed easily by the pumps. The motion was severe, but the ship had survived worse. Then the wind shifted northeast, setting up a vicious cross chop between competing northwest and northeast seas. The lightship was driven this way and that, unable to face the tumbling walls of living water bow on. The strain on her anchor chain was extraordinary and the little ship absorbed more and more punishment. The wind reached a speed none of the men had ever experienced before, heeling *No. 82* far over, exposing more of her upper works to the battering waves. The devil wind swung north and the assault continued. How it happened again is unknown, but it is fair to speculate that about now the mast went over, crashing either on the deck or into the water. The tin stack followed, leaving her without power of any kind. Flooding continued and without the steam pumps, lost when the stack went over, the crews only real hope for survival was for the storm to end quickly. The small yawl went over the side long before. There were no life rafts, but in the prevailing storm conditions, it made no difference to anyone's chance of survival. Life jackets were useless. Likely the men huddled together below decks and prayed for deliverance. There is an old saying that there are no atheists in foxholes. I suspect there are also none in sinking vessels in the midst of a freshwater hurricane! With a sudden lurch the mooring cable broke and the small lightship was at the complete mercy of the storm. The huge waves slowly battered the cabin to pieces, smashing in doors and portholes, knocking whole bulkheads clean off the vessel. Entire waves washed into the open decks below. Without a moments hesitation, *No. 82* dove for the bottom. What crewmen were still aboard were swept into the open lake like so much flotsam.

It was not until shortly after 3 a.m., on November 11, that genuine fear for the safety of the lightship was felt. The grain-laden steamer *Champlain* passed by where *No. 82* should have been but didn't see her anywhere. The steamer had been badly battered by the tumbling seas and barely struggled into Buffalo harbor.

The captain of the *Champlain* stated his fears for *No. 82* when he docked. Most marine men discounted them. After all, only one lightship sank at her moorings as the result of storm stress and that was out on the east coast. In August 1893, *Lightship 37* sank off Five Fathom Bank, New Jersey, when overwhelmed by a hurricane. Lightships just did not sink from storms. They rode them out. That's what they were built to do! Old-timers at the dock just felt she had been blown off station. She would be back anytime and when the crew hit town on liberty, they would have more stories to tell.

She never did come back to her old post. She was gone forever. Several days later a lifepreserver stenciled "Light Vessel *No. 82*" was found on the beach near the city. Other wooden wreckage confirmed the loss of vessel and crew. The only tangible clue to the loss was a small piece of wood on which a short message was hurriedly scratched, "good-by, Nellie, the ship is breaking up fast. Williams." It was surmised it was the captain's last words to his beloved wife. The body of the captain was found on the beach several days later. Almost a year later, October 29, 1914, the body of the chief engineer, Charles W. Butler, was found in the Niagara River, 13 miles from the site of the sinking.

The dead hulk of *No. 82* wasn't discovered until May 9, 1914. A U.S. Lake Survey vessel using a wire sweep snagged it in 63 feet of water, 7/8 mile north northeast from the old mooring. The hardhat diver that verified the wreck identification, reported the hull was still intact, but the interior was wrecked. He could see no bodies. The violence of the storm had evidently washed them clear of the hulk. The diver also said that her mooring cable had parted.

Reid raises No. 82. *The Reid tug* Manistique *is on the right and the steamer* S.M. Fischer *on the left. Credit: Huron Lightship Museum.*

The Reid tug Manistique *and steamer* S.M. Fischer *have No. 82 cradled between them. Note the steam pumps on either side of the wreck. Credit: Huron Lightship Museum.*

The lightship was raised on September 16, 1915, and later repaired and returned to service. Salvage proved harder than originally thought. The first contractor failed and it took the expertise of the legendary Captain Tom Reid to accomplish it for a fee of $19,500. Her station off Buffalo was unmarked until October 1916, when No. 96 was placed on the mooring. In June the following year the brand new No. 98 assumed the station.

This closer view shows the tremendous devastation the storm visited on No. 82. *Credit: Huron Lightship Museum.*

Later in Buffalo, curious people examined the infamous death ship.
Credit: U.S. Coast Guard

Old *No. 82* was rebuilt completely. All that remained viable from the original vessel was the hull. Considering the salvage costs, it was a very expensive proposition. During the 1916 season she remained laid up and from 1917-1925, served as the Tenth District relief ship. From 1926-36, she marked Eleven Foot Shoal in Lake Michigan until the station was discontinued. Declared surplus to the Service she was sold to the Boston, Massachusetts, Veterans of Foreign Wars, *USS Constitution* Post, and used as a floating headquarters. Her ultimate disposition is unknown. One source says she was scrapped in 1942; another that she was sunk by vandals in 1945.

Other lightships would eventually succumb to the powerful force of storm and gale. Less than five years after *No. 82* sank, No. 6, stationed at Cross Rip Shoals, Massachusetts, disappeared with all hands after being hit by a massive mountain of wind-blown ice. The vessel wasn't found for 15 years until a government dredge accidentally sucked up pieces of her hull some distance away from her moor. *Lightship 73* at Vineyard Haven, *Massachusetts,* perished with all hands in a 1944 hurricane. When the full furies of the storm gods strike, it makes no difference if it is lake or ocean. For a lightship there is no safe harbor and no place to run!

References:

Flint, Willard, *Lightships of the United States Government, Reference Notes* (Washington, DC: Coast Guard Historian's Office, 1989), np.

Putnam, George R., *Lighthouses and Lightships of the United States* (New York: Houghton Mifflin Company, 1917), p. 209.

Runge Collection, Wisconsin Marine Historical Society, Milwaukee, Wisconsin.

Chapter Four

New Buffalo Light

As explained in the introduction, the early days of lightkeeping on the Great Lakes or anywhere else in the country, were not a model of efficiency. Shoddy construction, building lights in the wrong places, "unreliable" keepers and pettifoggerish bureaucracy were all present. New Buffalo Light well illustrates these problems. It isn't that anything dramatic happened at the light. Nothing really happened at the light at all. In fact, the light itself probably should never have happened!

The light at New Buffalo, Michigan, on Lake Michigan's south shore was established almost by accident. The story goes that in 1834 the schooner *Postboy*, mastered by Captain Wessel Whitaker, wrecked on the shore about ten miles east of Michigan City, Indiana. To report the disaster, Captain Whitaker had to trek from the wreck to that city, via the long and sandy shore. During his journey he stumbled across the place where the Galien River entered the lake and decided in a flash of optimism that it would be a great place for a town. After he finished his business relating to the wreck, he returned home to Hamburg, a small town near Buffalo, New York and drummed up support for his idea. His salesmanship was successful and by 1835, the land was bought, surveyed and the town of New Buffalo established.

Of course every lake town needed a lighthouse and the founding fathers started to lobby for one. Obviously, New Buffalo would develop into a major port and it was only right the government built them a light. After all, nearby St. Joseph, Michigan, got one in 1831, Chicago in 1832 and tiny Pottawatomie Island at the entrance of Green Bay in 1836-37. Just down the lake, Michigan City received theirs in 1837. What about New Buffalo? Where was their light?

Responding to the lobbying of the good citizens of New Buffalo, in 1838, the government selected a site for the lighthouse. The actual location was on a sand bank 40 feet from the lake which, while visually effective, also assured a very poor base for any structure. The land in question was owned by Captain Whitaker who sold it to the government for a mere $200.

A contract was duly let with the same man who built the Michigan City light. Among other details, the light tower was to be built of hard brick or stone, round in form and 25 feet in height. The keepers house, also of stone or brick, was to be a 34-foot by 20-foot one-story structure with an attached 14-foot by 12-foot kitchen in the rear. Generally, it was a near twin to the Michigan City light, other than tower height.

The illuminating apparatus was to be a "Winslow Lewis patent" device with 11 lamps and corresponding 14-inch reflectors. By terms of the contract, the light was to be finished by October 15, 1839.

The contractor did not make the deadline. When he finally finished, the resulting work was so shoddy that water leaked through the tower dome badly enough to wet the lamps and reflectors. It was later suspected the inspection certificate was falsified by the government overseer. Only the threat of legal action by Stephen Pleasonton, the Fifth Auditor, against the contractor brought minimal relief with some repairs.

Poor construction standards were common to many of the early Great Lakes lights. The first Fort Gratiot light on Lake Huron was a case in point. The original 1823 contract called for a tower of quarried stone and Romain cement and a heavy stone foundation.

When completed though, it had become a tower built of beach cobbles held together with common mortar on a wood foundation. After every storm the resulting structure showed signs of falling apart. Mortar crumbled and cracks appeared in the tower. A creaky, narrow wood staircase climbed steeply from the ground floor to the third. A thin iron ladder provided access to the lamp room but only after crawling through a small and awkward scuttle door. The contractor neglected to build the first or second floor.

The brick lightkeeper's quarters was just as shoddily made. The brick was inadequately fired and when it rained, moisture soaked through, ruining the interior plaster and paint. Living in the lighthouse was a miserable experience.

The crumbling Fort Gratiot tower was finally put out of its misery in 1828, when a storm demolished it. Better attention was paid to the construction of the replacement facility. The new structure, finished in 1829, stands solid to this day.

The first New Buffalo keeper, Thomas S. Smith, was appointed by Pleasonton on January 3, 1840, at a salary of $350 per year. The light was first exhibited on June 20, 1840.

Numerous structure problems other than the leaking dome and bricks were quickly evident. One source called the lighthouse an altogether "Miserable concern." Building quality was very poor. Even worse than the inferior condition of the structure, the lamps were cheap and ineffective, a problem common to all Winslow Lewis appliances. Putting it all in perspective, the building was a disaster and the light could barely be seen by mariners.

Keeper Smith turned out to be a bit of a problem too. It later was revealed he lived 17 miles distant from the light and used a hired man to do the actual work of lightkeeping. In other words, according to the best of political tradition, he received the appointment and stipend as keeper and in turn paid another man to do the work for considerably less money, pocketing the difference. This was not unusual in the era of the infamous Fifth Auditor. The lightkeeper at St. Joseph was doing the same thing!

Left with little other choice, Pleasonton removed Smith as keeper in August 1841. The man recommended to replace him by the Lake Michigan Superintendent, was a fellow known only as Mr. Webster, who had lost both his legs in an accident. Pleasonton objected to the Secretary of the Treasury that such a man was obviously unqualified. Surprisingly, considering the politics of the times, he was not selected.

The second keeper was Elijah Pressey. Although evidently better than Smith or the legless Webster, not everyone in New Buffalo supported him. Early in 1843 Pleasonton received a petition from some local residents advocating the keeper be removed for neglect of duty. Apparently the complaint revolved around his frequent absence. Pressey was evidently able to answer Pleasonton's questions well enough to keep his job.

The problem of hiring competent keepers was common to this period on the lakes. For example, a July 20, 1842, letter from the Treasury Department to the district superintendent threatened to fire the Manitou Island (on Lake Michigan) keeper if he did not immediately improve. He was directed to cease using a hired man to keep his light for him, to move back into the lighthouse himself and to clear the trees blocking the light's visibility from the lake. Lightkeeping was often not viewed as a serious business but rather as a political reward almost of an "honorary" nature.

In the fall of 1843, the Lake Michigan lighthouse superintendent inspected the New Buffalo station and found it in a filthy condition. He felt the keeper had"... been very unfortunate in his choice of a partner, so far as housewifery is concerned." As explained in the introduction, although the husband may have been appointed keeper and charged to maintain the mechanism, tower and grounds, the house was the wife's job. The superintendent also noted the keeper was often absent from the light. Since the superintendent also commented the light was only used by ships possibly once a month, perhaps the keeper's attitude was, "Why bother?"

In another report on the lighthouse the superintendent stated, "The... (light)... is of no service whatever to navigation and is universally spoken of as a useless light. As the place at which the light is situated contains only a population of some twenty-five or thirty persons, affording neither commerce nor shelter for vessels, its abandonment cannot possibly injure anyone."

During these early years there was also a state of Michigan superintendent of lights. When he visited the light in June of 1845, he initially discovered the keeper absent. When he finally found him, he chastised him for not being at the light and the poor state of the lamps. Pressey promised to improve. When the superintendent returned in November, things were even worse and he recommended the keeper's removal.

Pressey was subsequently fired and Reuben W. Smith appointed in his place on December 20, 1845, starting a kind of musical lightkeeper game. Smith kept the position until July 27, 1849, when Joseph Miller was appointed in his place. On April 15, 1853, Miller was fired and Smith was reappointed. Although it is not possible to verify it beyond all question, it is quite reasonable to draw the conclusion that the changes in keeper were directly driven by politics. The "ins" fired the "outs'" men and appointed "their" men. Competence was not a part of the decision-making process. The free exercise of such petty political maneuvering was another characteristic of the early Fifth Auditor reign.

Smith was evidently an effective keeper or at least on good political terms with the Lake Michigan Superintendent, who noted during an 1847 inspection,"... an excellent light, everything in order, well kept."

For a very brief period, the light actually was a useful aid to navigation, but more by accident than deliberate planning. In January of 1847, the Michigan Central Railroad finished its line as far west as New Buffalo. Captain Eber Ward, the famous steamboat entrepreneur, in turn established a steamer connection between the town and Chicago. This useful period was short-lived. By 1850, the railroad reached Michigan City and soon after Chicago, ending the Ward Line steamer service to New Buffalo.

The original poor construction of the lightstation continued to cause problems. During an 1850 inspection it was noted the foundation of the building was giving way causing one side of the kitchen wall to partially collapse. The poor location of the structure had come back to haunt the Fifth Auditor.

The truly horrible Winslow Lewis lamp system original to the light was finally replaced with a sixth order Fresnel lens in 1857. The Fresnel remedied major problems with visibility, reliability and functioning. Of course the light was not of use to anyone, but at least now it could be seen if it was ever needed!

The New Buffalo Light was finally discontinued in August 1859. Recommendations for eliminating it were made as early as 1843, when a Revenue-Marine officer charged with checking various lights suggested the light be abolished. Another inspector stated, "It's abandonment cannot injure anyone." Pleasonton at first disagreed. After all, he just built it! Two years later the arguments had played out in Congress and it recommended discontinuance too. True to its political roots however, when opposition was raised to this local welfare program, Congress capitulated and the useless light continued in operation.

The official reasons for the discontinuance of the light were given as its proximity to the St. Joseph and Michigan City lights as well as the lack of vessel traffic to the town. It is worth noting that the identical conditions existed when the light was built! Today there is no sign that the light was ever there.

References:

Annual Reports, Lighthouse Service, various years, RG 26, NARA.

Gruse Harris, Patrica, *New Buffalo, MI Lighthouse,* 1839-1859 (Michigan City, Indiana: GEN-HI-LI, 1993), pp. 1-17.

Hawkins, Bruce, "A Miserable Piece of Work," *Michigan History* (July-August 1989), pp. 40-42.

Lighthouse Letters Book, RG 26, NARA.

New Buffalo Story, 1834-1976 (New Buffalo, Michigan: New Buffalo Area Bicentennial Committee, 1976), p. 10.

Vent, Myron H., *South Manitou Island* (New York: Publishing Center for Cultural Resources, 1973), pp. 46-47.

"Jump For It"

Rescuing shipwrecked sailors was not a part of a lightkeeper's job, not by a long shot! Sometimes though, the old wickies had to roll up their sleeves and do what had to be done. The wrecks of the schooners *J. C. Gilmore* and *A. P. Nichols* are cases in point.

Lake Michigan winds blew hard during the fall of 1892. Shipping everywhere on the lake felt the effect. Rough passages, blown out sails, time lost in shelter, all were commonplace as the result of the foul weather. There were problems off Pilot Island, too. While the schooner *J. C. Gilmore* was beating through Death's Door Passage on October 17, the wind suddenly shifted. Unable to tack, the schooner was blown on the island about 11:00 p.m. She ended up parallel to, and less than 10 yards from the wreck of the old scow-schooner *Forest*. Martin Knudsen, the lightkeeper at Pilot Island, and his two assistants jury-rigged a breeches buoy and stood by ready to rescue the crew. Since she was solidly on the reef and the schooner gave no indication of breaking up in spite of the battering waves, the crew wisely elected to stay aboard instead of risking the makeshift apparatus. When the weather calmed they did make it to the beach with Knudsen's help. The marooned crew hoped to borrow the keeper's sailboat to go the mainland for aid. The storm gods never did take a break and the lake continued to churn hard. Eleven days later they were still stuck on the island.

Pilot Island light station. Credit: U.S. Coast Guard

Since it was too rough to make even the short five-mile crossing to Washington Island, Knudsen still had his wife and two younger children with him. He sent his two older children to Washington Island before the fall storms rolled in to the area. He would try to get his remaining family over when the lake calmed.

Knudsen especially liked having his family with him since the island was an extremely doleful place. One historian claimed the only event that broke the monotony was when ". . . schooners were ground into wreckage on the neighboring reefs." Victor E. Rohn, keeper from August 1872 to November 1876, had been an officer in the Civil War. After spending a couple of years on the island he noted in his log for July 4, 1874, "Independence Day came in fine after a heavy southeast gale. This island affords about as much independence and liberty as Libby Prison, with the difference in guards in favor of this place and with the chance for outside communication in favor of the other."

Pilot Island stands squarely between Detroit Island to the northeast and the rugged west shore of Wisconsin's Door Peninsula to the southwest. The narrow channel that cuts just to the south, named "Port-des-Morts" or "Death's Door Passage" by the early French explorers, was a notorious ship trap. As dangerous as it was short, it is still the quickest way from Lake Michigan to Green Bay. Pilot Island received its name from its relationship to the notorious passage. A visitor in 1890 described the island as ". . . a little island of three and a quarter acres of rock and boulders on which there is an imported croquet ground, a few ornamental trees, a strawberry patch, two fog sirens, a lighthouse, a frame barn, a boat house and some blue, bell-shaped flowers and golden-rods that grow out of the niches in the rock." He, like keeper Rohn, wasn't impressed with it.

The combination of adverse winds and powerful and treacherous currents proved too much for many vessels. In the fall of 1872, the keeper reported eight large schooners stranded or wrecked in the passage in a single week. The previous year, a hundred vessels were lost or damaged in navigating the infamous "door." It wasn't uncommon for the keeper or an assistant to be trapped on Washington Island during a supply run for weeks before being able to return to the island. The true total of ships lost nearby remains open to speculation, but in the infamous October 16,1880, storm an estimated 30 vessels went ashore in the area. Waves ran so high they frequently broke over nearby Cana Island light. The lantern, 88 feet high, was inundated with spray from the smashing seas. One victim of that monster storm was the steamer ALPENA, lost somewhere in mid-lake with all aboard, an estimated 60-100 people.

The island's fog whistle was said to be heard 40 miles away and while sounding, all of the lanterns in the fog house had to be hung by cords or the vibration would extinguish them. The blasts were so powerful chickens couldn't lay and milk curdled in minutes. One wag claimed overnight visitors to the island on foggy nights where so startled when the blasts started, they leaped from their beds and started looking for their resurrection robes! By contrast, the keepers were so used to it, they barely even heard the blasts.

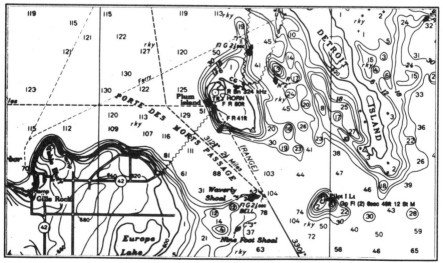

The infamous "Port des Mortes" passage.

On October 28, the winds kicked in extra hard and the veteran keeper knew more trouble was brewing. He could smell it on the wind. He warned his young assistants to keep their eyes sharp for any vessels in distress. Long experience told him that with weather this dirty something would happen and whatever it was, it would not be good!

From high in the tower galley the lighthouse crew spotted half a dozen vessels having a hard time of it. Some were able to work their way well clear of the reef. Several others were forced to anchor and came perilously close to the island before their anchors finally grabbed hard into the rock bottom. In at least two instances the stress of riding at anchor was too severe and they had to slip their hooks and beat their way out into deep water for safety.

Shortly before 2:00 p.m., the men spotted a three-masted schooner to the southeast, evidently trying to make her way through the deadly Port-des-Morts Passage into Green Bay. Thick snow squalls and stinging sleet storms swept through the area, periodically obscuring visibility and blotting the schooner from view. When the wind shifted from west to northwest, the big schooner could not hold up her course. Through gaps in the snow squalls, they saw her head for nearby Plum Island for shelter, a couple of miles to the northwest. Just about dark when she reached the lee of the island the captain let go her big 1,400-pound anchor with all the chain, a full 600 feet. This long scope would give the hook the best chance to catch in the rocky bottom. It wasn't to be. The big anchor bounced uselessly across the lake bed and the schooner continued inexorably toward Pilot Island's deadly reefs. Looking at her through his big telescope, Knudsen recognized her as the *A. P. Nichols*, a well-built and especially beautiful schooner. He had seen her many times before. A fast sailer, at one time she did a record trip, running from Chicago to Buffalo in three days and 16 hours.

The grim, dark outline of the schooner, head to sea with anchor chain streaming out into the depths, was sometimes glimpsed briefly by the lightkeeper when his beam flashed overhead. Usually though, the darkness, snow and sleet blotted out any glimmer of the ship. Whether they could see her or not, they knew she was out there somewhere and coming their way. They only had to wait.

Just after 8:00 p.m., Knudsen and his assistants were all in the cozy lighthouse kitchen enjoying a cup of steaming coffee. Keeper Knudsen wanted to give his men a quick chance to warm up and relax before sending them back out to search the storm-whipped waves. The peace of their brief respite was broken by a loud crash. The men dropped their cups and, accompanied by the keeper's wife Theresa, rushed out into the wild night. Illuminated by the thin, probing beam of the tower light was the big schooner, apparently so far ashore it looked as if the jib boom reached over the beach. When the men looked the situation over closer, they discovered it was indeed the *A. P. Nichols*, the schooner that earlier had been dragging her anchor and that she was alongside the wreck of the old *Forest*. The *Gilmore* lay 25 yards or so off her stern. When they looked closer, they saw the *Nichols'* starboard quarter had

The schooner A.P. Nichols *is on the right and* J.C. Gilmore *on the left. The ladder to the* Nichols *is supported by the old* Forest. *Credit: University of Detroit Marine Collections.*

ended up very close to the bow of the *Forest*. The *Nichols* was not fast ashore, but was still "alive," rolling badly every time a sea crashed into her and, with each roll, the hull ground down toward the *Forest*.

The 115-foot, three masted scow-schooner *Forest* had gone on the beach exactly a year before. Somehow losing her way in a southwest wind, she fetched up hard with her stern nearly ashore and bow extending into deep water. Storms later tore the old vessel apart, ripping out her masts and washing the cabin on the beach where it became a playhouse for island children. The deck remained on the hull, although barely above water level, running out into the lake like a long wooden finger.

After a quick conference, Knudsen and his men came up with a plan to rescue the *Nichols* crew. It was clear that from the terrific pounding of the schooner, she couldn't last long. Action was needed now! Knudsen and one assistant carefully climbed up on to the deck of the *Forest*. In the intervening year they learned the wreck well, knowing where the open hatches were and what part of the splintered deck could still bear a man's weight. The assistant, Hans Hansen, stopped at the land side of the schooner. His job would be to guide the survivors over the slippery rocks to shore. Knudsen continued on to the bow. There he wrapped one arm tightly around a pawl bit and leaned out in the blackness toward the *Nichols*. The *Nichols* stern quarter loomed a full 15 feet above the broken *Forest*. One slip and Knudsen would be in the water, certain to be ground to pulp between the two hulls. He hoped to persuade the crew to jump for it when the schooner rolled inwards. He would then grab each in turn and drag them aboard the *Forest*. The assistant would help them ashore. As loud as he could he yelled the plan to the *Nichols* crew. Yelling against the howling wind, crashing seas and grinding of the hull, it took several long minutes to have his plan thoroughly understood by the confused survivors.

Standing on the wind swept-shore with the second assistant keeper, Theresa could only silently watch and pray for the safety of her husband and the salvation of the crew. The blackness of the night that engulfed her was nearly total. Only when the piercing beam of the light rotated briefly overhead was she able to get a glimpse of the men working desperately on the old *Forest's* sunken deck.

The first man to risk the crossing was the captain, David Clow, Jr. As the *Nichols* rolled ponderously toward the *Forest*, Knudsen yelled, "Jump for it!" The captain leaped out into the black night but slipped on the wet rail and landed heavily in the water. Reacting instinctively, Knudsen grabbed him by his hair and heaved the sputtering man to safety. Together the captain and Knudsen schemed how to best recover the rest of the seven remaining crew, including a woman cook and the master's 320-pound father, Captain David Clow, Sr. The two men agreed to tackle the father next. Nearly helpless with infirmity, he would be the most difficult victim.

The sailors on the *Nichols* quickly rigged a rough rope harness around the old captain, then suspended a ladder down the hull toward the *Forest*. The hope was that elderly Captain Clow could climb down the ladder supported by the harness and at the proper moment, reach out to the *Forest*, where his son, the assistant keeper and Knudsen would haul him aboard. The first attempt failed. An unexpected wave sent the harnessed old sailor, ladder and all, flying into the air only to bounce back hard against the *Nichols* hull. On the second try he hesitated too long before stepping out to the *Forest* and nearly went into the water before the three men were able to grab him and, with tremendous effort, pull him aboard.

The superannuated captain, a veteran of many years on the lakes, had been wrecked on nearby Plum Island three times before. In June 1876 he went up twice, but each time came off without damage. On October 15, 1881, he went on the reef at the southeast end of the island with his schooner the *Lewis Day* after she broke her centerboard on some rocks. Initially the injury was slight. When the weather turned stormy she was destroyed by heavy seas.

One by one, each of the people remaining on the schooner was safely brought off and escorted to the warmth of the lighthouse's friendly kitchen, where Theresa presided over the coffee pot. Sitting safe and comfortable in the kitchen, the old captain reminisced about the wreck of the DAY when he realized with a start that Knudsen had helped with that rescue too! Tiring quickly from his ordeal, the old man was helped by his son and Knudsen to the room of the assistant keeper on duty, where he was bedded down for the night.

In the cold gray light of the following morning, sailors and lightkeepers together examined what was left of the schooner. The sails were blown to tatters, jib boom lay across her deck, masts broken, cabin roof ripped off and the stout hull shattered from grinding on the jagged rocks.

The survivors of the *Nichols* stayed at the lighthouse for nearly two weeks before the lake calmed enough to let them reach the mainland. Luckily the men were able to salvage some provisions, clothing and bedding from the schooner. The lighthouse keepers had little enough for their own use. Sharing with the *Nichols*crew badly depleted their meager resources, especially considering they still had the *Gilmore* crew to take care of, making a total of 16 persons. The stormy lake finally calmed enough for the keeper to use his small sailboat to take the young Captain Clow out to a steamer enroute to Escanaba. She in turn carried the news of the double wrecks to family and underwriters.

Knudsen's role in the *Nichols* rescue was recognized by the Lifesaving Benevolent Association of New York and the U.S. Government. The first organization sent the keeper a gold medal two inches in diameter. On the front was a scene of a schooner on a stormy sea and a lifeboat. On the reverse was the inscription:

"Presented to Martin Knudsen Light House Keeper on Pilot Island Lake Michigan in recognition of his courage and humanity in rescuing at

great personal peril the crews of the schooners J. R. Gilmore *and* A. P. Nichols *October, 1892."*

In the spring the lighthouse tender *Dahlia* brought the second award. After anchoring just offshore, the vessel's commander came ashore and formally presented Knudsen with the Second Class, also known as the "Silver," Life-Saving medal, for his heroism that terrible October night. The simple inscription hardly explained the terrible danger Knudsen faced and overcame.

"To Martin Knudsen Keeper Porte Des Morts U.S. Light Station For Services in Saving Life at Wreck of Schooner A. P. Nichols *October 28, 1892."*

An accompanying citation better explained the danger and achievement, stating that he was ". . . exposed to storm and darkness to the waves as well as the falling spars of the stranded vessel. . . "

Martin Knudsen came to Pilot Island in 1880, after the first assistant, John Boyce, committed suicide in June of that year. Knudsen left the following year to assume the duties of lightkeeper at South Manitou Island, a position he held until returning to Pilot Island in 1899. He remained at Pilot Island until 1896, when he moved with his family to nearby Plum Island, two miles to the northwest. Later he transferred to Racine, Wisconsin, and finally in 1917 to North Point Lighthouse at Lake Park, Milwaukee. He retired in June 1924, at 70 years of age. Knudsen lived for 19 more years, succumbing in July 1943, from complications of a broken hip. So ended the life of a true American lighthouse hero.

References:

Annual Report, United States Life-Saving Service, 1893, p. 197.

Adamson, Hans Christian, *Keepers of the Lights* (New York: Greenberg, 1955), pp. 321-322.

Hirthe, Walter M. and Mary K., *Schooner Days in Door County* (Minneapolis, Minnesota: Voyageur Press, 1986), pp. 33-42.

Holland, Hjalmar R., *Old Peninsula Days, Tales and Sketches of the Door Peninsula* (Madison, Wisconsin: Wisconsin House, 1972), pp. 232-242.

Knudsen, Arthur and Evelyn, *A Gleam Across the Wave* , pp. 56-63.

Runge Collection, Wisconsin Marine Historical Society, Milwaukee, Wisconsin.

Tragedy at Squaw Island Light

Squaw Island lighthouse was one of the most beautiful on the Great Lakes.
Credit: U.S. Coast Guard.

Squaw Island Lighthouse was at one time one of the most beautiful on the Great Lakes. Although the red brick building is long
abandoned and been heavily vandalized by a host of degenerates,
the vestiges of past glories are still present; a fine wooden staircase,
two bedrooms, dining room, sitting room, tile floors, spiral tower
stairs, watch room, lantern room and wrought iron galley railing.
The year "1892," the year of its construction, is cut into the corner-
stone. Today the island is privately owned and visitors are discouraged.

How the island got its name is open to speculation. One belief is
that Indian women who wanted to have children went to the island
as somehow the environment would magically ensure fertility.

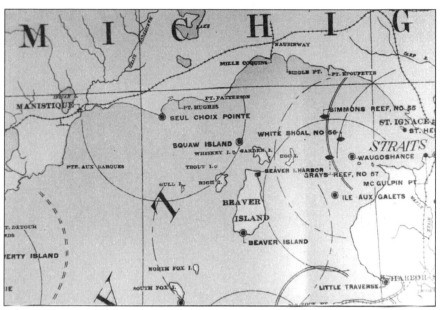

This chart from a 1910 circa Lighthouse Service Annual Report *shows Squaw Island and its relationship to other lights. Credit: Author's Collection*

Squaw Island, three miles west-northwest of Garden Island and four and a half miles north of Beaver Island, is the most northwestern of the islands west of Grays Reef Passage. The lighthouse is on the northern end of the island and was important in guarding the west edge of the shoal for vessels turning up or down from the Straits of Mackinaw. Its fixed red light with a flash had a 13-mile range. There was also a big 10-inch diaphone steam whistle for fog.

The waters offshore the island were the scene of a terrible lighthouse tragedy. In the early days, the Service made no provision for getting the keepers and their families onto the islands in the spring or off in the fall. This was strictly the individual responsibility of each keeper. Keeper William H. Shields had been at the light since the 1892 opening and knew the procedures well. When he received orders to close for the 1900, season, he and his assistants, Owen J. McCauley and Lucien F. Morden, loaded their 25-foot Mackinac boat with all of their needed household goods and waited impatiently for good weather. This was McCauley's first year at the light. Morden, a native of Montague, Michigan, had been a Squaw Island assistant since November 7, 1899. Guessing the best time to leave in the fall was always chancy, but on the morning of Friday, December 14, conditions looked good although it was bitter cold, so they hurriedly closed up the lighthouse and left. Also aboard were the keeper's wife and a niece, Mrs. Lucy Davis of Richmond, Indiana. McCauley was eager to get to St. James. His wife Mary was pregnant and her time was near. She stayed in St. James rather than accompany her husband to the light so she could be close to medical care.

When they pulled away from Squaw Island, St. James lay about eight miles to the southeast. With luck they could be there in a couple of hours. For a while all went well, with a frigid northeast wind driving them at a good clip. However, after a while the wind turned fluky, blowing alternately from different directions. A sudden northwest squall struck without warning and knocked the small sailboat over until her sails touched the water. Everyone but McCauley was dumped into the lake. He was quick enough to scramble over the gunwale and grab on to the centerboard strake. Shields struggled to keep his wife afloat and Morden held on to Mrs. Davis. Laying over on her side the boat still floated, although nearly awash. After a difficult struggle the men managed to first cut away enough of the rigging to get both women lashed to the boat, then do the same for themselves. There was not enough room on the overturned hull for any of the survivors to be completely out of the water. Their lower legs were left dangling in the lake. There also was no strength left to right the boat. The overwhelming cold was drawing out their last reserves of energy. Barely afloat, inundated by every wave and bone-chilled, the five desperate people continued to ride the waterlogged boat. As time passed, the two women grew more and more affected by the relentless cold. They shivered violently and were wracked with convulsions. Plainly they were reaching the end of their tethers. They had clearly lost hope and that was the worst of all.

McCauley later remarked, "The weeping and wailing of these innocent creatures through their untold suffering would melt the hardest of hearts. It is beyond my ability to describe the terrible scene and I prayed in silence for their sufferings to cease. What a pity."

Mrs. Davis was the first to perish. While suffering on the hull she had mentioned through chattering teeth that she came to Squaw Island because her doctor recommended going north for her health! Now as the result of following his advice, she would soon be dead. She knew her end was near. She was quiet for a long time, then softly sang the old hymn, "Nearer my God to thee." It seemed to comfort her. Shortly after nightfall, she silently died.

Sometime later Mrs. Shields became delirious, begging to be cut free and allowed to drift off into the waves. Her end was near too. Reluctantly her husband sliced the ropes and she slid off the hull into the water. About 8:00 p.m., she died.

Morden was the next to go. Although he was clearly of the water, sitting on the hull, he was drenched with spray and frozen to the bone. It was later thought that because he had spent much of his time at the light inside reading law, he lacked the hardiness of Shields and McCauley who spent their free time outdoors. Shortly after Mrs. Shields slipped off into the dark water, he too simply slipped into the welcoming water and death.

Shields was worse off than McCauley. The older man slipped in and out of delirium as the cold sought to pull him into darkness. To keep him alive, McCauley struck him with his fists and kicked him with his feet to keep him conscious. Shields at one point responded by telling him he would rather die naturally than by being kicked to death. But McCauley's kicks kept the old man alive.

Slowly the arctic wind blew the boat toward the shore. The two women were dead; one still lashed to the boat and the other drifting underwater at the end of a rope. Although Shields had cut his wife free of the hull, he had left her lashed to a trailing line. The two men clung to the thread of life. Just when it looked as if the wind would blow them ashore, it swung to the east and drove them back out into the lake. All that Friday and into the night the dead and dying continued to drift in the cold swell of the dark waves. Overhead the stars burned bright and cold in the heavens.

Finally, late Saturday morning they were delivered from their terrible ordeal. A sharp-eyed lookout on the Gilchrist steamer *Manhattan* spotted them. At first he saw only black spots on the water. The captain, J.C. Dobson, using his big marine glass, was able to make out what he thought was only wreckage from some unknown disaster. Then he saw the people. Swinging the big steamer around, he pulled close aboard and stopped, using the bulk of the steamer to break the force of wind and wave. Four volunteers from his crew rowed over in a lifeboat and gently cut the victims free, including the two dead women.

All the victims were brought aboard the ship. The men were barely alive. Rescue had come just in time. Hot soup and good whiskey helped restore them enough to be able to tell the dreadful details of the disaster.

When the steamer reached Manitowoc, Wisconsin, both men were rushed to the hospital. Local coroners quietly took the women's bodies away to the morgue. Although badly frostbitten, McCauly survived relatively well. His rubber sea boots and long woolen underwear had helped him greatly. After eventually recovering, he was later appointed keeper at Squaw Island, remaining until the station was closed in 1928. He then transferred to St. Joseph, Michigan, where he stayed until his retirement in 1936.

Shields did not fare as well. As the result of the appalling cold, a leg had to be amputated, one side of his body was partly paralyzed and his face halfway drawn out of shape. It was an appalling price to pay, but at least he was alive.

Shields' convalescence was long and difficult, physically and emotionally. The memories of the horrendous deaths of his wife, niece and assistant, certainly played hard in the dark recess of this mind. It is said he longed for death as a release from the pain that at least for a time, was nearly constant. He did eventually recover sufficiently for the Service to appoint him as the keeper of the supply depot at Charlevoix, Michigan. The actual work required was slight, as befit a man of such damaged health. His assistant did the real labor while Shields provided the supervision.

Unexpectedly the broken-down old lightkeeper also found romance. A young woman who had known both the keeper and his wife in better times, reacquainted herself with him during this frightful period. Love blossomed and soon they married. Reverend William H. Law, the famous chaplain of both the Life-Saving Service and Lighthouse Service, recalled visiting the couple in 1905. "I found him enjoying life as any ordinary mortal in a nice little home in a beautiful town on the green banks of a charming little inland lake, where he can care for his chickens and ducks and catch fish when he desires them and, apart from children, surrounded by all the comforts of domestic life."

It was a scene far different from the terrible time lashed to a waterlogged sailboat off the coast of Lake Michigan. Shields remained at Charlevoix until retiring in 1924. A year later he died.

Today the Squaw Island tragedy is nearly forgotten. This is very wrong in that it should remind us both of the appalling price often paid by the pioneer lightkeepers and their families and the constant danger of shipwreck of any kind on the Great Lakes.

References:

Author's Collection, Squaw Island File.

Biggs, Jerry, "Squaw Island," *The Beacon* (December 1995), pp. 12-14.

Farrant, Don, "Five Against the Lake," *Lighthouse Digest* (May 1997).

Law, William H., *Among the Lighthouses of the Great Lakes* (Detroit, Michigan: W. H. Law, 1908), pp. 13-14.

Register of Lighthouse Keepers, RG 26, NARA.

Runge Collection, Wisconsin Marine Historical Collection, Milwaukee, Wisconsin.

U.S. Department of Commerce, *United States Coast Pilot - 6, Great Lakes: Lakes Ontario, Erie, Huron, Michigan and Superior and St. Lawrence River* (Washington, DC: Government Printing Office, 1986), p. 265.

"That's' the Lighthouse, Hard Right!"

Lansing Shoal is certainly one of the most dangerous areas of northern Lake Michigan. Many vessels met their end on its deadly rocks. *The Great Lakes Pilot*, the bible of the shipping fraternity, identifies it as " . . . an extensive area of boulders with depths less than 24 feet, . . . from 4.4 to 6.2 miles north of Squaw Island. The shoalest spot, covered 13 feet, is at the southeast end of the ledge."

At first marked with a gas buoy in July 1900, the Lighthouse Board transferred Lightship 55 to the shoal when it became available in 1901, after the construction of the Simmons Reef lighthouse where it previously was stationed. Lightship 55 was one of the first three government lightships on the lakes. All three were built by using a back door approach to the problem of specific congressional authorization.

A March 2, 1889, Act of Congress provided $60,000 to construct a light on Simmons Reef. Located 16 miles east of Lansing Shoal, it

Lansing shoal lightship at winter quarters in St. Ignace, Michigan on December 15, 1907. Note the three lanterns at the base of each mast. Credit: U.S. Coast Guard

was a major hazard to shipping. This amount was grossly inadequate for the job and the Board asked for an additional appropriation. While waiting for the slow wheels of Congressional appropriation action to grind, the Board on March 3, 1891, authorized the use of the existing $60,000 to build three lightships designated Nos. 55, 56, and 57 to be stationed respectively at Simmons Reef, White Shoal and Grays Reef. These would be the first permanent lightships on the lakes. While this was not the exact purpose, the money was appropriated for it did, with a little stretching, meet the intent of the legislators.

The 129-ton vessels were 102 feet in length, 20 feet in beam and 8 feet, nine inches in draft. Smallish by ocean standards, each of the wooden ships was also equipped with a 100 horse-power steam engine capable of giving a top speed of eight knots, just powerful enough to allow it to move on and off station without the expense of a towing vessel. Cost per vessel was $14,225, considerably cheaper than a saltwater lightship. For example, Lightship 50, a 120-foot steel framed vessel built in San Francisco in 1892 for use on the Columbia River, cost a hefty $61,150. Since the lightships were only on station part of the year and they were only lakes after all, the Service thought they could make do with less capable vessels. It was an error not repeated.

The three original Great Lakes vessels were framed and planked with white oak, fastened firmly with 5/8 inch iron spikes. Each had two masts, the forward for the daymark and the aft for a small riding sail. The little tin stack reached skyward out of the diminutive deckhouse. Mooring was provided by a five-ton sinker and 15 fathoms of two-inch chain permanently positioned on station and buoyed. This arrangement eliminated the need and cost of the vessel carrying her own gear, resulting in greater cost savings and efficiency.

The three ships were intended as an experiment to avoid the high cost of permanent lighthouses. With an expected annual operating cost of $4,000 each, they were far cheaper than the $250,000 construction cost eventually spent for Grays Reef station, for example. The annual permanent station operating costs for items such as salary, oil, food and other supplies were in addition to any construction costs.

The illuminating apparatus for the lightship was a cluster of three oil burning lens lanterns for each mast. A six-inch steam signal and hand operated bell served as the fog signals. In 1906 a submarine bell was added.

A lightship fog bell. Credit: Author's Collection

The three vessels were not very successful. When Lightship 55 was delivered from the Blythe Craig Shipbuilding Company's Toledo yard and during her trials on October 2, 5 and 6, 1891, many building defects were noted and extensive repair and modification was needed. Whether the numerous problems were the result of shoddy work, or poor design was never clearly determined.

Lightship 55 is perhaps best known for deserting her post. During November 17-20, 1891, a mere 23 days after being placed on station at Simmons Reef, she left without orders and put into Cheboygan, Michigan. Lightship No. 56 at White Shoal and No. 57 at Grays Reef came in right behind her. Why the crews took them into port was not recorded. Judging however by her many problems, it is likely they experienced a bit of a "gagger" while on station. Seeing how their vessels reacted to the storm, they carefully considered their own proclivity for continued survival and decided discretion was indeed the better part of valor. Dropping their moor, they fired up their small engines and put into port. Probably the crews ended up in the nearest sailor saloon and recounted their close survival to anyone willing to listen. The crews were immediately fired and more "trustworthy" men hired. Apparently the lighthouse tender *Dahlia* then towed all three back to their respective stations and stood guard to prevent any additional desertions.

During the ensuing winter, yard crews worked to correct many deficiencies that were on the ships, including missing or faulty equipment and performed extensive modifications for crew comfort. After the work they were considered adequate, if not good vessels.

In 1901, after only 10 years of service, extensive dry rot was found in her frames and planking that required considerable and very expensive repair work. In 1920, No. 55 was retired from duty and two years later sold for a mere $840. The experiment of a low-cost alternative to a fixed tower was a failure.

Lightship 55 was replaced with Lightship 98, a 101-foot, 195 ton steel whaleback vessel built by the Racine-Truscott-Shell Lake Boat Company of Muskegon in 1915. This vessel stayed at Lansing Shoal until the permanent light tower became operational in 1928. While she never deserted her post as her predecessor did, she was struck by passing vessels in the fog twice, both times in less than a month! The first incident occurred on July 8, 1928, and the second on August 4. In each instance the damage to the lightship was minor, the steamer receiving the worst of the encounter. Lightship sailors greatly feared collisions. When two freighters hit each other, it was usually a collision between two moving objects. The lightship, however, was a stationary target making it comparatively easy to hit. Picture yourself standing on the deck of Number 98. Shrouded thickly in the clammy gray mist you peer anxiously into a world without definition. The melancholy blasts of the foghorn blow a warning to passing vessels to stand clear. Periodically your ears detect the answering blast of a passing vessel. Sometimes they were far away, or at least seemed to be. It was hard to tell with the distortion the fog gave sound. Other times their response was so close it seemed the ship would slam into the lightship immediately! It was always a very scary time.

Service-wide, a total of five lightships were sunk by collision. Fog was a factor in many collisions, but surprisingly, most happened during good visibility, the result of passing vessels not allowing for current or leeway.

There were major problems in trying to mark the shoal with a lightship. Often because of ice, it could not reach the station early enough in the season, or stay until the final close of the navigation season. In 1900, when the difficulties of using lightships to replace regular lighthouses were clearly apparent, the Lighthouse Board started advocating for the construction of a full permanent station on the shoal.

Lansing Shoal light station, circa 1945. Credit: U.S. Coast Guard

The present station became operational in 1928, making it one of the newest on the lakes. The massive concrete base is 74 feet square and 20 feet high. What made the station unique is that the crew quarters were built deep in the crib below as opposed to living in the deck structure which was more traditional. Light and ventilation for the crib spaces came through the portholes. All the machinery and other equipment were in the 32-foot square, concrete building on the open deck. The short 30-foot high tower stands 13 feet square at the base and 11 feet at the top. The original lens was a third order Fresnel with a focal plane height of 69 feet. When the Coast Guard automated the light in 1976, the Fresnel lens was removed and carefully placed on exhibit in the State Museum in Lansing, Michigan. A solar-powered 190 mm optic replaced it.

On following pages is an interview with Captain E. C. Baganz, a veteran Great Lakes master of widely acknowledged ability. When he retired in the 1960s he was the commodore of the fleet for U. S. Steel (Pittsburgh Steamship Company) and had accumulated 51 years on the lakes, 49 with U.S. Steel and sailed as a master for 36 of them. The subject of the interview is the story of Captain Baganz and his ship the *George W. Perkins* during the infamous 1940 Armistice Day storm and its very close encounter with the Lansing Shoal light.

The steamer George W. Perkins. *Credit: Author's Collection*

The *Perkins* was built in 1905 by the Superior Shipbuilding Company in Superior, Wisconsin. One of four sisters, when launched she became one of the biggest bulk carriers on the lakes. Other than the normal scrapes and bumps of the trade, the *Perkins* had an uneventful career. In November 1940, the *Perkins* was a very typical Great Lakes freighter in every way.

The storm that struck on Armistice Day, November 11, 1940, was one of the worst ever recorded on the lakes and certainly rivaled the notorious November 1913 tempest. As in the 1913 storm, the severity caught mariners by surprise. Throughout the storm temperatures hovered around zero and tremendous waves blasted the all of the lakes. Three of the ships mentioned by Captain Beganz were total losses. The 253-foot Canadian freighter *Novadoc* went ashore near Pentwater and eventually became a complete loss. The 420-foot *William B. Davock* with her crew of 32 men and the 380-foot *Anna C. Minch* and her crew of 24 foundered in the same general area with all hands.

The steamer William B. Davock. *Credit: Rutherford B. Hayes Presidential Center*

There were also many lesser casualties. On Lake Michigan, the steamer *Frank J. Peterson* went ashore at St. Helena Island, just west of the Straits of Mackinac. The *Sinaloa* fetched up at the Garden Peninsula and the *Conneaut* at Manistique, Michigan. Driven by the horrifying waves, the carferry *City of Flint* 32 missed the piers and drove aground at Ludington, Michigan. Two South Haven fish tugs disappeared with all hands, eight men good and true. On Lake Superior the big steamer *Sparta* went on the beach at the Pictured

Rocks, just east of Munising. A dozen other vessels throughout the lakes suffered major damage.

The Canadian steamer Novadock *was broken in two off Pentwater, Michigan. Credit: Author's Collection.*

The experience of Captain R.W. Parsons on the steamer *Thomas F. Cole* was perhaps typical of the that of many other ships caught in the maw of the storm. He departed Gary, Indiana, on southern Lake Michigan at 4:00 p.m., on November 10, upbound for the Straits. When he settled down on course, the wind was blowing 25 mph from the southeast and he had little concern for the weather bureau's storm warnings. By 10:00 a.m., the following day, the wind had increased considerably and with a falling barometer, he decided to run southwest for shelter. He was expecting the wind to turn northeast, which would give him a sheltered course to the Straits. The *Cole* made good weather of it until a series of massive waves lifted his bow high out of the water presenting enough sur-face area that the wind was able to blow the ship completely around so he was heading northeast. It was a turn of a full 180 degrees! The pilothouse crew was helpless to prevent it. The *Cole* did not have the power to swing back to the original course. All she could do was continue on the heading the storm wanted her to run on. The cold air caused steam to rise from the water, reducing visibility to a couple of hundred feet. Without radar, the steamer ran blindly on into the storm. Parsons battled the storm with all of his skill, keeping the old steamer out of desperate trouble. Around midnight a mammoth wave climbed over the stern and caved in the steel plating on the aft cabin, causing the telephone to fail. With the life-line already carried away, none of the pilothouse crew dared venture back to the galley for food or coffee and no cook would come forward. For 36 long hours they fought the storm without benefit of caffeine or sandwiches. After the storm moderated enough for a crew member to struggle to the galley, he was greeted by a scene of complete devastation. The heavy stove was broken to bits. The walls of stout oak paneling were smashed into splinters. The deck was covered by a sea of pots, pans, crockery and silverware. Everything was broken that could be broken. Topside the open weather deck was covered with a full foot of ice. It took all of the captain's skill as a ship handler to bring the *Cole* out of that terrible maelstrom of wind and sea. Later in port, he claimed so many rivets were missing from the hull it looked like a giant cribbage board! Captain Beganz's account follows:

Lake Superior may be the biggest of the lakes, but the worst waves I have ever seen were on Lake Michigan during the 1940 Armistice Day storm. They ran all the way up from Chicago the whole length of the lake.

It's quite a story, worst storm I ever had and I have had a lot of them. But they never bothered me. I thought this one was the end though! Fifty foot seas, I don't think any of them [Coast Guard] ever had that kind of experience.

We were coming down from the Straits [of Mackinac] and in the Fall you can come down by way of Grays Reef but usually its' around Lansing Shoals. Its' a little further to go but it's deeper. You don't want to get stuck by Grays Reef. Anyhow in the winter draft you are a little lighter, about a foot. The wind was southeast which meant its better to stay on the east side of the lake.

We went through Grays Reef OK and got as far as Point Betsie [Michigan]. The weather report came out, southwest going to northwest, whole gale. The whole gale was all right, but the wind didn't shift, it stayed south-southwest right up Lake Michigan.

We got down to Betsie, got their weather report. We're on the wrong side of the lake! We're on the east side and we should be on the west side! So we headed straight across for the Sturgeon Bay Canal [Wisconsin]. We got about 15 miles off the canal. By now we got to head into it of course. I got a bearing on Sturgeon Bay Canal indicating we were not making any head way. We're not going ahead, practically standing still! The seas were that strong! About 7:00 that night the wheelsman hollers, "I can't hold her up!" A loaded boat can't turn around easy. She started to turn around to windward. The wind was pushing her right around! I was up there [in the pilothouse] and jumped on the telephone and told them [the engineers] to give it to her. Little by little, with a hard over wheel, she came back around one by degree at a time. You could hear the gyro go tick-tick-tick, 14 degrees then 15 degrees back the other way. Finally we got around. That was a real battle!

By now we were up by Green Bay. Let's go in there as close as possible. It's pretty tricky to go in there. It's snowing like hell. You can't see a quarter of a mile. We can't find the entrance. What do we do? We got to go some place. So we headed her up for Lansing Shoals.

I had a Hallicrafters radio that you could receive on but not send. I had brought it up to the pilothouse to listen to what's' going on. They were reporting three ships gone down where I was at Point Betsie. Davock, Novadoc, Minch, *they were half an hour trying to find out if it was two boats or three. They kept confusing* Davock *and* Novadoc. *They were reporting winds of 100 with gusts to 125 mph. They were warning the hunters not to go north of Ludington, trees down, no telephones and Lansing Shoals Light was out of commission. Both Lansing Shoal and Grays Reef were out. Their boats were gone, they had four-foot of water in them and furnaces swamped. One boat, the* Harvey, *was in the same vicinity, somewhere near Seul Choix and she was in bad shape too.*

I said we will head for Lansing Shoal. We can't get a good course. Radar would have been handy to find out were you are but we didn't have any. We couldn't tell where we were, just really guessing because we were wallowing around so much. Finally we saw a light on the left-hand side where there shouldn't be any. But there it was. It's a flashing light. It can't be Lansing Shoals. We couldn't possibly be there yet. It was Gull Island, near where the Bradley *sank. I yelled, "Hard left!" We just pulled into a little bay and came right out. We never touched a thing. But the water was high, pushed all the way up otherwise we would have put her on the bottom for sure.*

Now we know where we are. Only 18 miles to Lansing Shoals. It's a Godsend! Maybe now we can make a pretty fair course. But it's still snowing like hell and we went to what we figured was short of 18 miles. At 15 miles we either see something or we turn around and head back into it again.

I was just about to try to come around when the lookout hollers, "There's a light over on the right-hand side!" It looked like a steamboat. You couldn't see a quarter of a mile. Everything was really only gray blur in the snow. Holy smoke! Everyone [in the pilothouse] says it looks like a steamboat but what is a steamboat doing out here? Well, what are we doing out here? I hesitated because I didn't want to go across his bow. My best bet was to turn to the right. I didn't want to turn the other way because north of Lansing Shoal is all rock. So I hesitated and as I hesitated the whole loom flashed like a blur. I yelled, "That's the lighthouse, that's the lighthouse, hard right!"

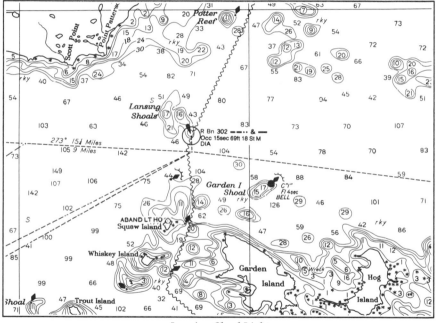

Lansing Shoal Light.

I just missed it with the steering pole. At a quarter mile, making about 12 mph, that ain't very far. I just missed it with the steering pole and now the stern is coming up. We are down in the trough of the sea and the sea is pushing the stern up. I opened the door of the pilothouse and looked back and there is the stack up in the sky and the lighthouse and it's coming right down on to the *lighthouse. That's when a miracle happened. The back-wash hit the lighthouse, bounced back hit us in the stern, gave us a rudder effect and we just slid by. That was close! That's why I say the lighthouse saved my ship from going on the rocks and I saved the lighthouse by not hitting it.*

The extreme danger the vessel was in is clearly apparent in the distant, academic words of the *Great Lakes Pilot*. "Lansing Shoals Light, 69 feet above the water is shown from a square gray tower on the south side of the 13-foot spot; riprap extends 50 feet from the base of the light, and it should not be passed close aboard even by shallow draft vessels."

In 20 minutes we were safe under Garden Island. The Farrel, *one of our Pittsburgh ships, was also anchored there. He had two anchors down, 90 fathoms on one and 80 fathoms on the other and going ahead under the island and the wind blew him back five miles. But it gave me a space to slip in. I went right up to the shore and dropped the hook right on top of a tree. The water was high of course and the wind blew it down into the deep water but I tucked in just as close as I could.*

One feller was washed right over Grays Reef. He thought he was on Hog Island next to Garden Island. The Coast Guard at Beaver Island came out in a boat looking for him since he reported he was at Hog Island. When they boarded my boat, they first went to the galley for breakfast. Them fellers knew where to get a good feed. Then they came to the pilothouse with great big binoculars to look for him. Hog Island wasn't far away and they could see from the pilothouse he wasn't there. They finally found him on St. Helena Island way up in the Straits. The wind had washed him over the shoals and everything.

When I got down to Chicago they [the company] told me they had to put 175,000 rivets in that boat [Perkins] that winter to replace the rivets that were loose or popped in the storm. That's how hard she worked in those big waves. You go down to the tunnels during a seaway in a pretty good storm, you don't want to go on deck so you go through the tunnels. The creaking and groaning, twisting scares the hell out of me. You want to get out of there, not to get trapped there. You wonder will she stand it, working so hard.

That was a worse blow than Fitzgerald ever got into. I don't think 1,000-footers could stand up to a sea like that.

Captain Beganz spoke of the damage to the upper lake lights from the terrific storm. The simple act of just reading the official Lansing Shoals Lighthouse journal sends chills up your spine. At the time of the storm, only two men, keeper G.L. Gordon and third assistant W.L. Keller, were at the light. The first and second assistant were at Beaver Island on leave. The punctuation is original.

November 10, *Sunday general duties. Moderate S to SE wind, clear.*

November 11, *Armistice Day. Barometer has been going down all day 4:10 p.m. 28.10. Tightened all port holes and put extra fastenings on south door of engine room. 6 p.m. both glasses in store room port holes broke out. 6:30 p.m. south door tore away, filling engine with water and put out fire in heating boiler. [Remember that the deck is a full 20 feet above the water, making the waves a minimum of 25 feet] Pulled all switches on electric and equipment everything out of commission. Called USCG and told them to report station out of operation. I believe it is now blowing 80 mph and cold with some snow.*

November 12 *12 midnight, it is blowing just as hard, very steady, about 60 mph and getting colder. Crib is icing, ice all over. 8 a.m. What a night we had. This morning everything is washing around in engine room. The south door is over in the north entrance as near as we dare to go is the landing on the stairs and it is awful to see. Every sea coming in and ripping something away and stirring it up with the rest of the wreck. 12 noon. Not blowing as hard as it was but plenty hard, and the wind seems to shift a little from the SSW to the west, and a heavy sea rolling from the SW. 6 p.m. the wind is going down some and hauling more to the WNW, but it is a hard breeze yet and there is not as many seas rolling in through the door. 9 p.m. wind NW and plenty strong yet and very cold. We have been 27 hours without any fire and I think I can get one going. Every sea that rolls in goes up to the grates. 9:30 p.m. Got the fire going but got all wet and I am cold. Got some more coal in fire and steam is starting. Not so many seas coming in door now, and our quarters is getting warm.*

November 13, *12 midnight. There is about a foot of water on engine room floor and we are working on Kohler No. 2. It is the only one that has a gas tank. The gas tanks on the other motors has broken away. 4.00 a.m. Kohler going and tower light going and using standby flasher. 7 a.m. Looking over the deck in daylight. I find one south door tore off. 2 porthole glasses in south end of engine room out. 2 in storeroom and 1 in 3rd assistant Keller's bedroom gone. Some stores gone out of store room which I haven't had time to check. All motors full of water. Gasoline tanks has a lot of water in them. Also distillate tank and kerosene tanks has lots of water in them. Both radio transmitters and generators got wet all the loose boards on transmitter floor floated off. There is* *about 4 to 8 inches of ice on all windows and doors. Got out north window and chopped ice off of north boathouse door. Moderate NW, clear.*

November 14, *Putting glass in portholes only had 7 on hand. 6 p.m. Tender* Hollyhock *arrived crib. Radio electrician looked over transmitter and found them OK so started them going but ice has the antenna grounded and we have radio B on steady to try and melt the ice off antenna. Light NNE and clear.*

November 15, *Beaver Island Coast Guard arrived at station 10 a.m. with 1st and 2 assistant and left 10:30 a.m. with Keeper and 3rd. Station sure is in bad shape. Moderate to brisk SW, partly cloudy.*

It is worth realizing that when Captain Beganz and the *Perkins* so nearly "clipped" the light, neither Gordon or Keller had the slightest idea tragedy was so close aboard. Both keepers were huddled deep in the concrete crib trying to wait out the unholy maelstrom outside. Imagine the reaction if either man looked out a porthole as the big steamer suddenly slid by. Would the man have believed what he saw, or just passed it off as a sort of apparition, another Great Lakes ghost ship?

References:

Annual Report of the Lighthouse Board, various.

Interview, Captain Edward Beganz, nd.

Bowen, Dana Thomas, *Memories of the Lakes* (Cleveland, Ohio: Freshwater Press, 1969), pp. 264-275.

Flint, Willard, *Lightships of the United States Government, Reference Notes* (Washington, DC: Coast Guard Historian's Office, 1989), np.

National Maritime Initiative, U.S. Department of the Interior, *1994 Inventory of Historic Light Stations* (Washington, DC: Government Printing Office, 1994), p.181.

Nelson, Donald L., "Lansing Shoal Lighthouse and the 1940 Armistice Day Storm," *Beacon* (September 1996), pp. 20-24.

Parsons, Captain R. W., "The Storm of 1940," *Inland Seas* (Spring 1996), pp. 22-25.

U. S. Department of Commerce, *United States Coast Pilot - 6, Great Lakes: Lakes Ontario, Erie, Huron, Michigan and Superior and St. Lawrence River* (Washington, DC: Government Printing Office, 1986, p. 265.

Van der Linden, Reverend Peter J., ed., *Great Lakes Ships We Remember II* (Cleveland, Ohio: Freshwater Press, 1984), pp. 263-264.

St. Martin Island, A Keeper's Life

The lighthouse at St. Martin Island at the upper entrance to Green Bay, is one of the newest on Lake Michigan. Built in 1905 on the northeast end of the island, the light has the only pure exoskeltal tower on the lakes. Six-sided, the steel structure soars 75 feet, giving the light a focal plane height of 84 feet. The lens was a fourth order Fresnel flashing red and white, with the white visible for 23 miles and the red for 19 miles. Besides the unique tower, there is a two-story brick keeper's quarters, fog signal building and oil house. A boathouse and dock were on the north, or sheltered end of the island. In the middle of the last century the island was home to both fishermen and Indians. A small cemetery near southwest bay has quite a few gravestones with names and dates of the 1860s and 1870s.

St. Martin Island lighthouse with its unique tower. Credit: U.S. Coast Guard

The wooded and hilly island is roughly 1350 acres in size. The coast is mostly rock-bound and steep. The keepers of the light and their families have been the only people living on the island in modern times and the station was only open from roughly April 1, until early December. The light marks the west side of the St. Martin Island Passage that runs between Gravelly and Gull Islands on the east and St. Martin Island on the west. The route can be used both to enter Green Bay and as a short cut to the ore port of Escanaba. Always dangerous to mariners, St. Martin Island Shoals run 1.5 to 2.3 miles south of the island. The shallowest spot is a bare seven feet. Rock Island is roughly 4.5 miles to the southwest and Washington Island at the tip of Wisconsin's Door Peninsula, two miles beyond.

Louis Bouchan shown in his Lighthouse Service uniform. Credit: Bouchan Collection

Mr. Louis Bauchan of Cheboygan, Michigan, is one of the last of the old-time lightkeepers. He became a lightkeeper almost by accident. During the Depression, he found himself working 12 hours a day for the A & P food stores for the princely sum of $5.00 a week. Seeing a newspaper advertisement for lightkeepers, he applied, took the required civil service test and ended up as number 12 on the merit list. Before he realized it, he was a lightkeeper! His career included service at St. Martin Island, Poverty Island, Chicago Harbor, Pilot Harbor and Point Betsie, as well as two stints on the icebreaker *Mackinaw*. During the Korean War he was stationed in Hawaii. He was a keeper at St. Martins from November 1, 1937, until April 1947. During most of his career, he was a member of the civilian Lighthouse Service, only transferring to the Coast Guard towards the end of his St. Martin time. His memories of life at the island, recalled during the interview, speak simply and eloquently of the commonplace situations and daily convenience we frequently overlook today.

Chickens and More Chickens

I went to Escanaba shopping one day and happened to go past a place selling chickens, $4.00 for 50 chicks. So I bought 50 chicks. When I got back to the station the other men laughed like heck. I put the chicks in a big box in the living room. We had no living room furniture so we were living out of the kitchen. I kept the chicks in the house only a few days, just long enough for me to build a little brooder shack outside for them. I ran an extension cord to that shack and a 25-watt bulb was enough to keep them nice and warm, just like a mother would have. Out of 50 chicks, I ended up with 46 that survived. Half were hens and the rest roosters. Soon we were getting all the fresh eggs we needed. Early in the fall I processed the roosters except one and that was the hardest thing for me to do. They were my friends. I guess I fed them right as *they dressed out just about five pounds each. They were all heavy breeds, white rocks, red rocks, etc. The wife and I pressure canned them and we had quite a few quarts for the following year. I made a deal with the guy from Washington Island. I said you take the hens over the winter and keep the eggs and it worked out fine. The next spring we got them back and had them the second year too. I eventually gave them all to him. The dwelling had a large, deep basement with a cement floor and we would put all our leftover canned goods on the floor and cover them and they were always good the following year.*

Rough Water

Just getting to and from a remote station like St. Martin Island could be very difficult. The following describes a simple trip to Washington Island for supplies. Remember, too, that Bouchan was running in relatively sheltered Green Bay, not the open lake.

I had some awfully rough rides. Washington Island was where we went for mail and supplies. It was about a 10 mile trip. A couple of times there was really some tough sailing.

One time we were getting low on groceries and one of my men was ashore. We had a crew of carpenters working out there and we were really almost out of groceries. I thought well, I'll take a run in and get my man and pick up groceries at the same time. The wind was south-southwest and I was on the northeast side of the island. When I rounded the right side and got into it, it was pretty wild.

It was a rough trip going in. It seemed like the winds were getting stronger all the while so when I got to Washington Island, I told the guy we would stay overnight. Maybe the wind will drop by morning. It's really rough out there. I called the station and told them we wouldn't be back till next morning.

The next day it didn't seem so bad out. The wind was in the same direction but it seemed like it dropped a little. I figured we could go out as far as Rock Island any how. You have Washington Island, then about two miles out there's Rock Island, then St. Martin Island another eight miles or so out. So I thought we would go as far as Rock Island. Then if its too bad there cause we start to get into the rough part we can turn around and head back to Washington Island. We got out there and it was really bad. I turned around to see what it was like coming at us and boy it was really rough! I said we made it this far, might as well go the rest of the way. Tie everything down. It was like riding a surfboard the rest of the way. We would get on top of a wave and I'd have a heck of a job holding her stern into the seas. That was the fastest trip I ever made out to St. Martin Island!

I got out to St. Martin and had to go around the island to the station side because I couldn't even land. Although the boat dock was in the lee, there were big swells coming in and the one man and I couldn't handle the boat to put it on the track to pull it out of the water. I had to signal the rest of the guys from the station to come down to the dock and help bring the boat in. The men got the car into the water and when there was a lull between the waves, I made a run for it and got it on the dolly.

The keeper at Poverty Island Light, which was on the south side of the island and got the brunt of the weather, called over and said no man should be out there today in a small boat. That ride was a rough one!

The boat was a 20-foot open one with an enclosed pilothouse. I had the throttle lever right by the wheel so I could handle both with one hand. I could speed up or slow down and it kept us going.

Old Lighthouse Service vs. New Coast Guard.

In 1939 the Coast Guard absorbed the old Lighthouse Service. For the old time civilian keepers it was a traumatic affair. Bouchan's account continues:

> There weren't too many of the keepers from the old Lighthouse Service that enlisted in the Coast Guard. If they did, they enlisted and retired right away. At Rock Island, Poverty Island, Minneapolis Shoal, Plum Island, they all had the choice of enlist in the Coast Guard or stay civil. Those near retirement age enlisted then retired right away. If you stayed a civilian you had to stay until age 65. In the Coast Guard you had 20 years and out. So for the old-timers it was easier to enlist and then get out.
>
> When the Coast Guard took over there was a lot of paperwork. In the old Lighthouse Service if you got one letter a month you were lucky. But after the Coast Guard took over, why instead of the little country mailbox that we used to have for the old Lighthouse Service, I had to build a box about [indicated roughly two feet square]. Every time you went for mail that thing was half-full with all their crazy literature. Boy, there was a lot of paperwork!

Aboard the SUMAC

Before becoming a lightkeeper Mr. Bouchan worked a stint as an assistant cook on the lighthouse tender *Sumac*. Even then there was a rivalry between the Lighthouse Service and Coast Guard. The following incident occurred during the 1935-36 period as the vessel was entering St. James Harbor at Beaver Island, Lake Michigan.

> The cook and I were getting ready for supper. We were standing in the galley watching forward out the door and I said, "Hey, we should have made our turn here." I no sooner said that than BOOM, we hit bottom.

The lighthouse tender Sumac *aground at Beaver Island. Credit: Bouchan Collection*

We piled on pretty hard. After a couple hours of trying to back off we had to put out a call for help. The old Coast Guard cutter Escanaba *was at Grand Haven [Michigan] and our sistership, the Lighthouse Service tender* Hyacinth *was at Sturgeon Bay [Wisconsin]. They both got our message so it was a race to see who would reach us first.*

This was the old lighthouse days so we were pulling for the Hyacinth *and she had a little shorter distance to go. When they got there she was all rigged up for towing already; they came up, put the two lines aboard us and pulled like heck. Finally they got us off just as we could see on the horizon the* Escanaba *coming up. We had to tell them to turn around and go back home!*

The Car

To provide some form of motorized transport Bauchan arranged to bring an old car to the island piece by piece. Every time they made a supply run to Washington Island, they returned with part

115

of the car. Finally they had all of the pieces and assembled it, converting it to an ad-hoc flat bed truck in the process. It served them well for many years.

Mrs. Bouchan and their son ready to go in the "car." Credit: Bouchan Collection

I'll tell you how handy the car came in. Before we closed up in the fall of '41, we had pulled the station boat up on the beach in the southwest harbor because the water was so low we couldn't get it in the boathouse. We used a double block and tackle tied to a tree and just heaved it up. Then the war started in December '41. In early March of '42, before the 15th, they ordered us out because they wanted to get the iron ore moving and a lot of the light stations opened up early. Usually we opened April 1

The Coast Guard took Dave Kincaid [another keeper] and I out. They dropped us on the ice at the southwest bay where out boat was and we walked ashore. We carried all our supplies to the beach and put all of them into the boat. It was late afternoon before we started to walk across the island, a distance of about two miles. No one had been at the island all winter and the snow was a foot and a half deep all the way. We had a heck of a job walking across. We only got about half way when Dave, who was heavy-set, he must have weighed 250 pounds or better and 63 years old, he said, "I got to rest. You go on ahead and get the fire started. I'll come in later on" I got to the lighthouse and got the fires started. We had an old fashioned coal stove in the living room and a wood range in the kitchen. Well, I got them both going. About an hour and a half later, Dave made it across and we settled in for the night.

The next morning it was a nice spring-like day. We had a workshop on the island with double doors at one end so I could drive the old car in for the winter. I had put it in there up on square gas cans for blocks under the axles. Before I let the car down, I wrapped some old logging chains through the spokes of the rear wheels for traction. We started out with a couple of snow shovels and Dave sitting on the back for weight. It took two hours to break trail across the island. Every once in a while we would have to stop and shovel snow away from the radiator it would pile up so deep. Finally we made it across to the boat and loaded up our stuff. It only took about half an hour to get back to the station. That car came in so handy!

When the families came out in the summer we would use it to get to the beach. There was a nice sandy swimming beach at south bay and on our day off my wife and kids and I would take the car over there and go swimming. We had the beach all to ourselves. The beach at the station was all large limestone with no sand at all. It was too hard on your feet to go swimming.

1940 Armistice Day Storm

Captain Beganaz in the Lansing Shoal Light story tells a spellbinding narrative of being out in the infamous 1940 Armistice Day storm. Keeper Bauchan had a different view of the storm. Remember, though, that Bauchan at St. Martin Island was in the lee of the southwest winds and thus relatively protected.

> Boy that 1940 blow was quite a storm. One ship tried to come into Green Bay and was coming around St. Martin Island to pull in behind us to rest out the blow. She made a big turn, came in and dropped her hook but the wind was so strong it kept pushing her out. So pretty soon she had to go out and make another big turn and come in again. Boy those waves were so high! It was a 600-footer and when she went up in the air I could see about a third of her keel sticking out of the water! The one piece of damage that storm did to the station was take away a little dock that we had labored so hard to build in 1939. Due to the fact that our regular dock took heavy seas from the north and northwest, we decided to build a dock on the beach right in front of the dwelling on the east side of the island. It came in handy several times. In the summer of 1940 we decided to add another 12 feet or so to it. We built a crib about 12 feet square and about five feet high up on the beach. It was getting late in the summer and into early fall so we decided to leave it until the next year before we would float it out and fill it with stones. That storm from the southwest must have raised the water level of the lake quite high because the day after the storm we had no dock there and the crib had vanished, all we had left was the broken end of the rope tied to the

tree. I heard later that the crib had washed ashore high and dry on big Summer Island to the east, northeast of St. Martin Island. Maybe it is still there. That storm cured us of trying to build a dock.

Today St. Martin Island is long abandoned. The old light station buildings echo now only with the quiet memories of the men who so well served the shining beacon.

For a while gasoline was delivered to the island by contract aboard a steam powered tug. In spite of the danger, the old tug never blew up! Credit: Bouchan Collection

Painting the tower was an annual job for all keepers. Credit Bouchan Collection

References:

Gilmartin, ET1 Joseph P., Sr. (Ret), "The Lightkeeper's Light," *Shipmates*, (October 1994), p. 7.

Interview, Mr. Louis Bouchan with author, March 5, 1997.

National Maritime Initiative, U.S. Department of the Interior, *1994 Inventory of Historic Light Stations* (Washington DC: Government Printing Office, 1994), p. 205.

"Pages From the Past," [*http://www.biddeford*.com/com/lhdigest/march97/bauchan.htm].

Upper Peninsula Sunday Times (Marquette, Michigan), July 29, 1979.

US Department of Commerce, *United States Coast Pilot - 6, Great Lakes: Lakes Ontario, Erie, Huron, Michigan, and Superior and St. Lawrence River* (Washington, DC: Government Printing Office, 1986), p. 340.

The Poverty Island Treasure

A lost treasure in gold and an old and forgotten lighthouse is a wonderful basis for any story, especially one that just might be true. The concept just seems to fit together doesn't it? It would certainly be more logical, however, in the old pirate cruising waters of the Caribbean Sea than in Lake Michigan. In any case, here is the tale and a tall one it is. Regardless of how wild, there are believers and perhaps with good reason.

There are many different versions to the story of how the treasure was lost in the first place and later salvage efforts. Here are some of them.

Version one involves an attempt during the Civil War to smuggle gold provided by Emperor Napoleon III of France to the Confederacy. Ostensibly it was to finance war supplies. Instead of trying to run the Federal blockade into a southern port directly which was considered too risky, another method was developed. Critical to the plan was finding a trustworthy captain able to bring the treasure across the stormy Atlantic and on down the Great Lakes. After much searching, a man was located and sworn to deepest secrecy. The gold was carefully packed in five stout wood chests and taken clandestinely to Canada, then loaded into a small schooner in a lake port. The schooner in turn was to smuggle it to Chicago, where it would be shifted to a canal barge and finally taken by riverboat down the Mississippi to the rebels. When exactly this all occurred is unknown, but it had to have been before the 1863 fall of Vicksburg and the resultant closure of the Mississippi River as a secure Confederate waterway. In any case, the secret of the gold transfer in the Canadian port must have leaked, because off Poverty Island in Lake Michigan, the ship was set upon by Great Lakes pirates. Since such brigands did not commonly cruise the lakes, they must have either trailed the schooner from Canada or learned of the cargo in sufficient time to allow them to race ahead and lay in wait. Rather than let the treasure fall into the hands of the pirates, the captain of the gold vessel chained the chests together and dumped them overboard into shallow water, intending to return later and recover them. Apparently, angered by losing the gold, the pirates murdered the crew and burned the schooner, thus destroying all evidence and witnesses. In pirate lingo, dead men tell no tales!

The second version claims the incident happened during the French and Indian War. The treasure was being carried on a French vessel and it was intended to purchase trade goods to buy the Indians loyalty from the British. When the vessel was attacked off Poverty Island, the captain also chained the chests together to avoid capture and consigned them to the deep.

The third version claims it was a military payroll shipped during the War of 1812. Again, after a pirate attack, it was chained and dumped into shallow water off Poverty Island.

The fourth version says it is really "King Strang's" gold. James Strang, the self-proclaimed "king" of the Beaver Island Mormons, was murdered on Beaver Island in 1856 by two disgruntled followers. Beaver Island was on the Michigan side of the lake, about 50 miles to the east. Supposedly he had a strongbox filled with gold, the result of his flock's offerings. Somehow in the confusion after his death the strong box ended up off Poverty Island.

The fifth version involves the Civil War but in a reverse fashion. During the final days of the conflict a big shipment of gold bars was in enroute from Lake Erie bound for a Chicago bank to be smelted into coins. The gold had been looted from southern banks, thus there was a cloak of secrecy over the entire affair. Instead of carrying it as precious cargo on a fast passenger steamer where too much attention would be paid to it, the gold was packed into a large wood chest and loaded as deck cargo on a barge carrying barbed wire. Although no date is given, the shipment was likely made in 1864, based on the collapsing state of the Confederacy and relative opportunity for bank theft. It could have been looted by

Poeverty Island light station, circa 1950. Credit: U.S. Coast Guard

advancing Union forces or by the rebels. Realizing the end of their nation was near, dispirited and defeated Confederates could have taken advantage of the chaos to loot their own banks. Either group would have been anxious to get it to a safe location. In any case in the fall of the year a tug towing a barge was steaming west through the Poverty Island Passage, bound for Big Bay DeNoc, intending to shelter there from a rolling northeast gale.

Lighthouse keepers were required to note any vessels passing their light and to this end, the assistant keeper at Poverty Island closely watched the tug and barge through his marine glass. He noticed the barge was low in the water, likely as the result of water

124

washing over the decks and finding its way into the bilge or even opened seams from the wave action. Approximately a half-mile north of the island the barge started to sink. Quickly the tug dropped the hawser and ran alongside. The tug crew leaped aboard the barge and cut the lashings of a large chest on deck then pushed it overboard. Their job done, they scrambled back aboard the tug moments before the barge sank.

Supposedly the following spring the tug returned with a derrick barge and divers and recovered the wire cargo. The lightkeepers watched the activity closely. Poverty Island is a lonely place and any human activity must have drawn the closest scrutiny. The fate of the mysterious chest is unknown. Several years later the light-

Poverty Island assistant keeper's quarters, circa 1913. Credit: U.S. Coast Guard

house keepers noticed salvage vessels again at the site. Curious about the activity, one of them rowed out to the tug, only to be ordered away after learning that the operations were under the direction of a Chicago bank. Several days later the salvers left. For years afterward, salvage vessels frequently returned to the area. Again, there is no record of the big chest being found.

T. D. Vinette of Escanaba, Michigan, has perhaps the best first-hand knowledge of the legend of the Poverty Island treasure. A commercial diver for many years, after a stint in the Navy during World War II, he opened a highly successful boatyard in Escanaba. In the spring of 1936 Vinette was working on a bridge project in Oconto, Wisconsin, when he was approached by Sol Meyer of Milwaukee with an offer to participate in the search for the treasure. Meyer had tried to hire a more experienced diver, but the man had broken his arm in a bar fight and was unavailable. He in turn recommended Vinette to Meyer as a good man for the task.

The Milwaukee man approached the young Vinette and explained the job. Vinette remembered: *I was a commercial diver and I dove for cash. The guy wanted me to go shares. I said no, cash only. I think I was the only man ever to make money on the treasure! So I came back to Escanaba after the bridge job and looked up a friend who was an historical buff. I asked him if he had heard of the story and he said, yes and told me his version. He said why don't you go and talk to Sheldon Cobb, he was a deckhand on the old Eleven Foot Shoal lightship that used to be off Peninsula Point. I knew Sheldon. We were neighbors as kids. He sent me down to Jessen at the grocery store. His father, who was an old Poverty Island lightkeeper, had died by now and his son was running the store. All of them had parts of the story. It seemed to be the consensus that there definitely had been an occurrence of a tug hauling a barge seeking shelter behind Poverty Island in a northeast blow and some deck cargo went overboard. So I thought maybe there is some merit to this thing.*

I had first heard about the Poverty Island treasure in the '20's from commercial fishermen. I used to spend summers in Nahma where my uncle was a fishermen. We would go to Little Summer Island bass fishing. Poverty Island is only five miles away and one of my cousins told me about the gold and people looking for it.

Meyer meanwhile returned to Milwaukee. In late June he agreed to Vinette's terms, $60 a day on days underwater and $10 a day for standby days, plus five per cent of all gold recovered. Vinette also agreed to arrange to charter a tug.

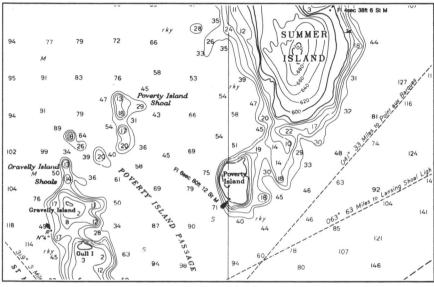

Poverty Island.

Operating from the 53-foot fish tug F.S. HOWARD, Vinette and others used a wire sweep to scour the lake floor in the area of earlier salvage activity. On the fifth day of the search they located the wreck of a 100-foot long wood barge in 55 feet of water, west of Poverty Island. Vinette was not able to identify the barge and at Meyers' request tore a plank off it. The fastenings that secured the plank were forged square spikes with small square heads. The Milwaukee men believed this meant the barge was of the right age. There was nothing of value on the flat-deck barge, but nearby Vinette discovered several bales of barbed wire. Vinette remembered, *When we found the wire the two men from Milwaukee were elated! Meyer asked me to bring up a bale of the wire. I took a pry bar down and dug out a roll of the rusted wire, tied it off to a line and it was hauled up to the surface. The guy with Meyer was an historian of some sort. He identified it as an old fashioned western wire, cow wire, with big single barbs three inches long. He thought finding the wire was just the most wonderful thing.* After considering the wind direction and lightkeeper's observations and the likely drift of the barge, they determined the enigmatic chest should be farther towards the shoal. Their search was fruitless. Other than finding a small anchor, they came up empty-handed. The anchor was roughly 100 pounds and attached to it was a length of very rusted 5/16 inch chain. The tug men believed it was from an old steam gill netter that sheltered behind the island in a southeast storm.

Supposedly in 1932, a freighter anchored in the area assisting in the salvage of a stranded ship. When it hauled its anchor up, one fluke was caught in a rusty chain which in turn was fastened to several wood chests. Before the crew could get them aboard, the old chain broke and they fell back into the depths. The same experience reportedly happened to the steamer ETRUTIA in 1904. She had anchored in the vicinity to wait out a fog. When it cleared and she hauled her anchor it, ". . . had caught the cable chain of a vessel, as well as some wreckage and a chest, which sank as soon as it appeared on the surface." A piece of the chain was saved which the captain believed came from a vessel of 400-500 tons. Another story tells of a steamer aground on the west side of the island. In order to free themselves, the crew used a boom to throw an anchor aft and haul off. On one try the boom came up with a chain hooked on a fluke and a chest dangling from it. Before it could be brought aboard, it slipped off and sank back to the bottom. Since the crew had no knowledge of the treasure, they thought nothing of it. Only later when one of the men related the incident to someone ashore, did someone put the story together. Are these all the same incident or different ones?

Another connection with Poverty Island light came about in the middle to late 1930s when a Chicago group was in the area with the vessel *St. Lawrence* equipped with a diving bell. The bell was reportedly nothing more than a 55 gallon drum with a view port cut into the side. It was rumored the group had a $35,000 nest egg to finance three summers of searching. The story goes that the lightkeeper's son was on the beach watching the general activity on the boat when the bell broke the surface and several objects were brought on deck. All aboard the vessel began to yell and scream, apparently in wild celebration. Later that night a storm blew up sinking the boat and killing several of the people, or so the tale is told.

Vinette remembered the vessel under a different name. When he was on the tug looking for the treasure, the two Milwaukee men asked him if he had ever heard of the *Captain Lawrence*. Vinette replied that, ". . . when we were kids she used to lay down at the merchants dock; a real derelict, a piece of junk. That thing lay there with two-three guys around it practically all of one summer. It was a little mysterious because they were talking about treasure. They didn't say where it was or how they were going to get it. One day she just disappeared from the dock."

The story continues that some years later, the diving bell washed ashore on Poverty Island after a fierce storm. For several years the lighthouse children played in the old bell, using it as a private hide-away all their own. One spring when they returned to the island, the bell was gone, apparently washed back into the lake. It has never been seen since.

In 1994, a company named Fairport International Exploration entered the picture with the purpose of finding and salvaging the treasure. Some estimated the potential value of the gold today at $400,000,000. Fairport based its claim on the following rather tenuous reasoning that runs along the plot line of an Indiana Jones film. In 1932, Milwaukee salvage diver Wilfred H. Behrens purchased the two-masted 65-foot schooner yacht *Captain Lawrence*. The vessel had a checkered past. Originally built in 1898, it was rebuilt in 1919 as a gas screw with the addition of a gasoline powered engine. In 1924 it was sold to the Milwaukee Boy Scouts and used as a training ship. At this point it received the name *Captain Lawrence*. In 1931 it sank in Lake Michigan and was subsequently raised and towed into shallow water in a Milwaukee river. When Behrens bought it for $150 it was certainly in near derelict condition.

In August 1933, the vessel left Milwaukee with Behrens as the captain and a crew of four. Their destination was Summer Island, just to the north of Poverty Island. On September 19, the vessel stranded on some rocks near Poverty Island, then sank after a "terrific wind came up." All the men reached the safety of Poverty Island with the assistance of lightkeeper Nels Jensen and his assistants. When contacted by the Coast Guard the next morning, Behrens declined salvage help. In the official Record of Casualties, it was declared a loss of $200 and to have no cargo. To put this in proper perspective, if the vessel was new the loss would have been closer to $14,500. Considering the purchase price of $150 and the loss of $200, any improvements must have been minor.

Fairport believed the *Captain Lawrence* and *St. Lawrence* was one in the same vessel and that it holds the key to the gold. After locating a propeller blade and an anchor thought to have been from the salvage vessel, Fairport arranged to obtain the rights to the vessel from a surviving heir of Behrens.

In June 1994, Fairport filed an admiralty action in district court seeking to, "perfect its title and salvage rights in the wreck," which also included the rights to 12.5 square nautical miles of bottom land, arguing that their the wreck may have scattered considerably, thus they needed the large amount of terrain.

To a degree the issue turned on whether the vessel was ever actually abandoned. Fairport claimed it never was and that Behrens heirs still held all rights to the vessel and its secrets.

The State of Michigan intervened under the Abandoned Shipwreck Act (ASA) of 1987 and filed a motion to dismiss the Fairport claim. Under the ASA the federal government asserts title to certain historic wrecks then transfers it to the states on whose submerged land the wreck is located. Michigan claimed the wreck met the requirements of the act and that therefore it belonged to the state.

The court examined the case closely. It noted that the *Lawrence* was a recent wreck and did not sink in deep water but rather stranded in shallow water. It further noted that the wreck is in pieces close to shore in 40-60 foot depths and was well within the salvage capability of the 1930s. Modern technology was not essential for finding the wreck or recovery.

If Behrens wanted to salvage it he easily could have. He continued to salvage dive for 10 years following the wreck, but apparently never returned to the wreck, nor did his crew. When Behrens died in 1959 he left no secret papers concerning the *Lawrence* to his family nor did they ever pursue the wreck or the supposed treasure. The court decided the vessel had been abandoned, hence the rights could not be conveyed to Fairport. On appeal to the 6th Circuit Court this judgment was upheld. Fairport was given no rights to the *Lawrence*.

The Poverty Island treasure tale has also been the subject of a 1994 segment on the NBC television program, *Unsolved Mysteries*. Richard Bennett, a Wauwatosa, Wisconsin, diving store owner, has spent 19 years and over $100,000 of his own money searching for the gold. He has used a variety of methods, including a sensitive magnetometer but finds an old-fashioned towing sled the best. Exhaustive research convinces him the treasure, perhaps worth as much as $400 million, is really there and just waiting to be discovered. The NBC program quotes him as saying, "I'm going to continue until I find it or someone else does."

So where does this leave the five boxes of gold?

Presumably it is still there, off the old Poverty Island lighthouse, somewhere near Poverty Island Shoal and just where the light-keeper's daughter (or son, or assistant keeper) saw the old-time divers celebrating.

Approaching Poverty Island by water. Note the lamp room has been removed from the tower. Credit: U.S. Coast Guard

It is interesting to speculate if somehow the Poverty Island light-keeper ended up with the gold. Maybe he ventured out to the site where the men pushed the box off the barge and grappled it up himself. Realizing a sudden display of wealth would only cause trouble, he hid the gold on the island and bided his time, finally resigning his position and moving far away to enjoy his newfound riches. Behind he left a legend and legions of searchers looking for what wasn't there.

The Poverty Island treasure story is one that never seems to end. There is always another twist. As I was finishing this piece, I came across a man who had searched for the wreck in the 1970s with a small submarine. He claims to have interviewed the grandson of the daughter of the lighthouse keeper. The grandson remembered her as definitely confirming the salvage of the gold in the years following the sinking of the barge. The recovery was kept secret. He also learned the wreck of the ST. LAWRENCE was just offshore in about 30 feet of water, on the west side of the island and north of the Lighthouse, about three-quarters of the way up the shore.

What then is the truth of the Poverty Island treasure? Is it fact, fiction or fancy; a strange tale whose details change to suit the storyteller?

Poverty Island Light Station was built in 1874-75. Located on the southwest tip of the island, its steady beam guided ships through the Poverty Island Passage into Green Bay. The original tower was a 70-foot brick structure, connected to a single-story brick keeper's house. In 1976 the light was moved to a skeletal steel tower.

References:

Action Shopper (Marquette, Michigan), September 14, 1981.

Barada, Bill, "The Treasure of Poverty Island," *Skin Diver Magazine* (March 1969).

Columbus (Ohio) Dispatch , [*http://www.treasure*.com:80/ 20296.htm].

Paul J. Creviere, Jr., *Wild Gales and Tattered Sails, The Shipwrecks of Northwestern Lake Michigan From Two Creeks Wisconsin To Dutch John's Point,* Michigan and All of the Bay of Green Bay (Paul J. Creviere, 1997), pp. 338-344.

Door County Advocate. July 16, 1904.

Fairport International Exploration v. The Shipwrecked Vessel, et. al., No. 95-1783, 6 Cir.Ct. (1997)

Fairport International Exploration v. Shipwrecked Vessel Capt. Lawrence, No 95-1783, Crt of App, 6 Cir. Ct., 1997.

Great Lakes Shipwreck, [*http://www.treasure*.com/80/n1,htm].

Grand Rapids (Michigan) Press , [*http://www.treasure*.com:80/ n19.htm], March 9, 1997.

Great Lakes Log, (May 1, July 1995).

Green Bay (Wisconsin) Advocate. May 29, 1851; July 22, 1852.

Green Bay (Wisconsin) Press-Gazette. September 19, 1933.

Inland Seas, (Summer 1995), p. 42; (Summer 1997), p. 113.

Interview, Mr. Richard Bennett, November 10, 1997.

Interview, Mr. T.D. Vinette, January 22, 1998.

Kozma, LuAnn Gaykowski, *Living at a Lighthouse, Oral Histories From the Great Lakes* (Great Lakes Lighthouse Keepers Association, 1987), pp. 93-101.

Milwaukee (Wisconsin) Journal. October 30, 1994.

Mining Journal (Marquette, Michigan). November 11, December 18, 1994.

National Maritime Initiative, U.S. Department of Interior, *1994 Inventory of Historic Lightstations* (Washington, DC: Government Printing Office, 1994), p. 194.

Nor'Easter, (July-August 1994).

Bob O'Donnell, "The Last Word," *Association for Great Lakes Maritime History Newsletter* (September-October 1995), p. 8.

Register of Keepers, Poverty Island Light Station. RG 26, NARA.

Sacramento (California) Bee. March 10, 1997.

Treasure Ships of the Great Lakes, (Detroit, Michigan: Maritime Research and Publishing, 1981), p. 21.

T. D. Vinette. "Search for Gold: 1936, Poverty Island Passage," *Soundings*, pp. 3-13.

Chapter Five

The Lighthouse That Wasn't; Superior Shoal

Lighthouses typically are built to warn mariners away from dangerous areas, to enable them to stand well away from rocks and shoals. But sometimes they weren't built and sailors needed to exercise the greatest caution without the help of the friendly beams of a warning light. Superior Shoal is a case in point.

Lake Superior is of course the biggest, deepest and roughest of the Great Lakes. When sailing well offshore, in what could be considered the middle of the lake, the last thing a sailor worried about was shoal water, at least until August of 1929 and the official discovery of Superior Shoal. The men who were present remembered it as a wonderfully warm and calm day as the U.S. Lake Survey vessel *Margaret* was taking routine cross-lake soundings. The Canadian Hydrographic Survey had earlier charted their side of the lake out to the 100-fathom line and the U.S. Lake Survey had finished the water south of the international border. A large gap remained in the middle and the *Margaret* was working to fill it in. All was considered deep water so there was no urgency attached to the job. It was just a routine, "filling in the blank spot." Captain William Green commanded the *Margaret* while Harry F. Johnson was in charge of the survey operation. Both were long experienced at their jobs.

To help mark the course, a series of "brush" buoys were set at three-mile intervals on a line from Manitou Island at the tip of the Keweenaw Peninsula to Passage Island just to the north of Isle Royale. The sounding line was run perpendicular to the buoy line, northeastward to the Canadian coast.

The expedient brush buoys were made from small trees cut on Cove Island, Ontario. A quarter of the way from the bottom several cedar blocks were wired to the trunk to help keep the tree floating upright. A line from the bottom of the trunk ran to the lake bottom. Several concrete blocks served as an ad hoc anchor. Different colored flags at the top of the trees provided a distinctive marking system.

During one of the survey runs, Robert C. Hanson was operating the electronic depth finder, a new instrument to the Lake Survey. The machine steadily indicated depths of 600-900 feet, exactly what was to be expected in the middle of Lake Superior. All was boring and very routine, just another day verifying what everyone knew, that Lake Superior was damn deep! Inexplicably the "pip" on the depth finder suddenly jumped to the top of the scale, before falling back into the expected deep water range. The only one who noticed the strange reading was Hanson who was closely watching and noting the readings for later plotting on a field sheet. Hanson immediately yelled to Johnson, but he didn't think it was important, probably just a glitch in the new-fangled machine anyway. He refused to turn back for another look. Hanson, however, persisted and eventually Johnson relented, telling Green to come about and retrace the course. At her normal survey speed of 12 miles per hour, the *Margaret* had already traveled a considerable distance from the strange sounding.

Hanson's claims were validated when they again spotted the unknown shoal with the fathometer reading 45 feet before falling off to 400 feet plus. After dropping a buoy on the high spot, they continued with the planned survey. Since the shoal was in

Canadian waters, a detailed survey was not their responsibility. That job would be left to the Canadians. When they reached port, Johnson notified Canadian authorities of the discovery.

The following year the Canadian Government Steamer Bayfield completed an exhaustive charting of the area. What she discovered was cause for considerable alarm! The shoal was determined to be roughly two and a half miles long and a mile wide. The shallowest spot was a bare 21 feet deep and about 100 feet in diameter. About three-quarter mile to the southward was a 30-foot spot. Obviously it was a great danger to deep draft vessel. Even a smaller ship plunging in a seaway could be smashed on such a shallow reef!

When the crew of the *Bayfield* came back to port they told some interesting stories, comments that did not make it into the official report. In one shallow spot the tallow in the sounding lead didn't bring up the expected gravel or sand. To the men on the *Bayfield*, the bottom seemed more like a wreck than a reef. When they pulled their grapple through the area, it snagged something that yielded, more like the standing rigging of a vessel. Although they tried several times, the grapple couldn't hold it and kept slipping off. Later they managed to grapple an ax to the surface. To the men on the survey vessel, it looked new and undamaged. It obviously had not been thrown overboard from a passing steamer because it was broken! The crew were certain they were working over the hull of a wrecked steamer laying on the slope of the shoal. Was it one of the missing French minesweepers lost in 1918, or the long gone *Bannockburn*, the big steamer that sailed into a "crack in the lake" in 1902?

Located 38 miles from the Slate Islands, the shoal was right on the Passage Island-Michipicoten Island steamer course! The upbound Soo-Passage Island course was only 17 miles to the southwestward and the Soo-Battle Island course 14 miles to the northeast. Clearly the shoal was in a very dangerous location.

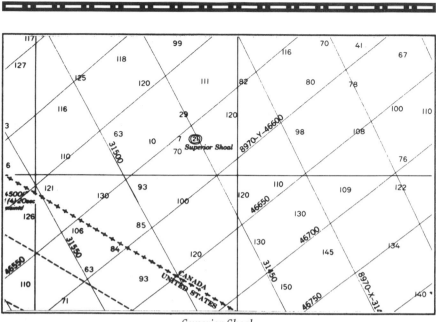

Superior Shoal.

Superior Shoal was first marked by spar buoys in 1934 and later by whistle, bell and radar reflector buoys. None could be made to stay in position. The mountainous waves of Lake Superior were just too powerful. Eventually all "walked off" into deep water and sank. Efforts to hold a buoy on the shoal were discontinued in 1954.

Although steamer men knew nothing of the shoal, American fishermen apparently had learned of it sometime earlier than its official discovery by the *Margaret*. When the *Bayfield* surveyed it in 1930, the crew were startled to see the big fish tug *Columbia* from Eagle Harbor working it. They also found fish nets set in 11 fathoms strung over the western part of the reef. The tug hastily departed the shoal before the *Margaret* men could question her.

Marine men sought a permanent lighthouse on the shoal, but their pleas fell on deaf Canadian government ears. Ministry officials claimed that it was impossible to permanently moor a gas lighted whistling buoy on the forlorn shoal. "How could they not build a lighthouse?" The *Toronto Sun-Times* newspaper didn't accept the ministry excuse for inaction, complaining that, "It is a serious reflection on the Marine Department that the general opinion among marine men is that if this reef were in the United States waters an up to date lighthouse and fog alarm would be built perhaps similar to Spectacle Reef on Lake Huron or Stannard Rock on Superior. . ." But in the end nothing was done. It was strictly a case of mariner beware.

What caused the strange storm that struck the Leafield? *Credit: K.E. Thro*

The discovery of the shoal did explain some mysteries, or at least presented a line of reasoning that could be contrived to explain them. In 1909 the 245-foot Canadian steamer *Leafield* was steaming in the area upbound for Fort William with a load of steel rails. The weather was perfectly calm with blue skies and a glass-smooth lake. Since everything was so tranquil the captain had already started to remove the tarps from two hatches in preparation for a quick turnaround at the dock. Without warning the lake blew into a terrific maelstrom. Waves crashed into the ship from every side. But there wasn't a breath of wind! Instead it was as if the lake was percolating from below, that the force was coming from the bottom of the lake. For almost half an hour the steamer was attacked by the strange storm. As quickly as it came, the fury subsided and the lake resumed its millpond demeanor. When the crew reached port they read of an earthquake that had struck and concluded that maybe they had sailed over a long dormant volcano that was affected by the shifting of the earth's plates. After all, they had been sailing over one of the deepest spots in the lake. The charts said so!

What did the Emperor *hit? Credit: Runge Collection*

Some years afterwards, the 525-foot steel steamer *Emperor* was upbound in the same area when she had another unusual "experience." The steamer was having a problem with its coal fuel and the captain stopped the ship in mid-lake to allow the engineers to clean the fire grates. The weather was calm but to prevent undue rolling and make the dirty job a little easier for his engineers, he added additional ballast to the side tanks. Suddenly the steamer bumped hard on something, then quickly slid off the unknown object. The ship's officers were at a loss for an explanation, after all the charts showed a hundred fathoms of water! To all appearances they had hit something, but nothing was there!

The big steamer *James S. Davidson* was downbound in the same region when an unanticipated heavy wave smashed hard into the bow. The shock of the impact released both anchors. Thundering out unchecked the chains snapped when they reached the bitter end, sending both anchors hurdling to the bottom, as well as damaging the hawse holes. Water flooded in through the injured area. When the D*Davidson* finally reached the Soo, she was severely down by the head. Had she encountered a storm, she well could have sunk. After being dry-docked, the amazed yard workers looked at a massive ten-foot dent in the bow. Clearly the *Davidson* had struck something very, very hard. Since the charts showed more than 100 fathoms where the incident occurred, what could it have been?

During World War I, a dozen 145-foot minesweepers were built at Fort William for the French Navy. In November 1918, three left in convoy for the Soo. A short time after rounding Passage Island a roaring gale struck the trio. Only one ever made it to the Soo. The missing two, complete with 32 man French Navy crews, had disappeared. Their loss is still unexplained, unless perhaps Superior Shoal is considered.

In the early 1920s the steel steamer *Midland Prince* reported striking something in the same territory. Again the charts showed the ship was in deep water and very deep water at that. Obviously the officers of the steamer were mistaken. You can't hit what isn't there!

Was Superior Shoal part of a long extinct volcano suddenly thrust up from the bottom by that 1909 earthquake? Could the shoal have been there all the time but no one ever noticed? One thing is certain however. A lighthouse was needed, but never built! It was the lighthouse that wasn't!

Were the two French minesweepers victims of Superior Shoal? Credit: Author's Collection

References:

Annual Report of the Department of Marine, 1931.

Canadian Hydrographic Service, Correspondence with author.

Environment Canada, correspondence with Author, March 29, 1976.

Hanson, Robert C., "Discovery of Superior Shoal," unpublished manuscript.

Landon, Fred, "The Discovery of Superior Shoal," *Inland Seas* (Spring 1959), pp. 50-54.

Notice to Mariners, No. 54 of 1930, Dominion of Canada.

Snider, C.H.J., Schooner Days, *Toronto Telegraph*, CII, August 26, 1933.

U.S. Department of Commerce, correspondence with author, May 23, 1973.

Woodford, Arthur M., *Charting the Inland Seas* (U.S. Corps of Engineers, 1991), pp. 121-123.

"Where is the Lambton?"

Throughout the years, efforts to survey the lakes were continuously made. As a result dangerous reefs and shoals were located and safe channels marked. Slowly a uniform system of lighthouses, buoys and charts were developed. The lighthouse, however, was the key to the entire system. It was on its reliable beacon that the sailor bet his life. Keeping the light became an important business. On the outlying stations, those on remote islands or shoals, keepers frequently battled heavy storms and gales that threatened to blow over the tower. In some cases the storms prevented the resupply of food and fuel and starvation became a real possibility. The result was it became a fight just to personally survive, let alone keep the light burning.

Often just getting the keepers out to their stations in the spring was especially difficult and dangerous. The tragic case of the lighthouse tender *Lambton*, lost with all 22 souls aboard on April 22, 1922, is a case in point.

The work of the lighthouse tender was unglamorous but critical. On the American side of the lakes vessels like the *Marigold, Dahlia, Amaranth* and *Warrington* delivered the keepers and their supplies to their lonely posts when they opened in the spring, kept them supplied throughout the season and returned for them at the close of navigation. On the Canadian side this duty fell to a tough little tug named the *Lambton*.

The *Lambton* was built in the Canadian Government Shipyard at Sorel, Quebec, in 1909. At 108 feet overall, 25 feet in beam, and 13 feet in depth, she was a small vessel for Superior's gales, but over the years she proved to be well-found and seaworthy. Twin engines and propellers provided excellent maneuverability and reliability, important attributes for a lighthouse tender. Passenger cabins on her main deck were used for lightkeepers and their families. Technically she was referred to as a "lighthouse supply and buoy vessel." Together with her sister ship *Simcoe*, she was responsible for navigation aids in the Canadian side of Lake Huron, Georgian Bay, Lake Superior and sometimes Lake Erie. The *Lambton* was homeported out of the Department of Marine and Fisheries station at Parry Sound on Georgian Bay.

The Lambton *on left,* Simcoe *on right. Credit: Ministry of Transport*

The larger, 180-foot *Simcoe* was built in England in 1909. The *Simcoe* ran with the *Lambton* until the 1917 season when she was sent to the Bay of Fundy on the Atlantic coast to replace another vessel that proved inadequate for the job. She was underway to her new assignment when she foundered in a severe storm with all hands on December 7, 1917, in the Gulf of St. Lawrence. Unlike the *Lambton*, the *Simcoe* did get a final message off. "SOS sinking condition SW Magdalen Islands or by few miles exact position not obtainable should judge about 10 miles southwest Magdalen Islands now clearing away boats heavy sea running SOS." A steamer and a naval patrol boat attempted to conduct a search but were forced back by the smashing seas. All 44 people aboard perished. No reason for the loss of this staunch and well-found vessel was ever determined.

Lambton's last trip began without fanfare. She left the Canadian Soo at 10:30 a.m., Tuesday, April 18, 1922, in the company of two

Playfair steamers, the *Glenfinnan* and the *Glenlivet*. The *Lambton's* task was to place the lights at Parisian Island, Caribou Island and

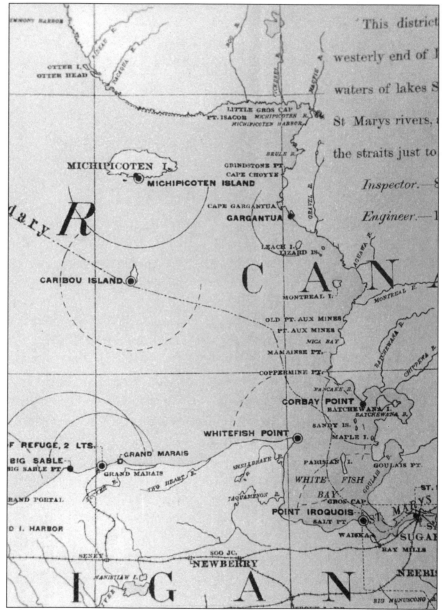

The Lambton *was likely lost somewhere near Caribou Islan. Credit: Author's Collection*

Michipicoten Island into operation. To that end, she carried aboard the keepers and their seasonal supplies. Including the crew, 22 men were on board the steamer.

In the cold spring air the keepers were likely tucked away in the warm deck cabins especially built to carry them and their families. Some napped, others played cards or perhaps even started a letter home. Large amounts of supplies were piled everywhere. On the decks were boxed food, clothing bundles, bagged coal for the steam boilers and drummed fuel for the lamps. All the supplies were stacked in separate piles for each light station to speed landing ashore.

At the time, heavy northwest gales were sweeping across Lake Superior and blinding snow squalls were reported in some locations. In addition, the strong winds had packed drifting ice into Whitefish Bay, an area that had been previously free of ice.

At 8:30 p.m., on April 19, the Soo was buffeted by a severe windstorm out of the northwest. The *Lambton* was known to be out in the Lake, and concern for her safety began to grow among local marine men. On the 20th and 21st, inquiries as to her whereabouts were made without result, until the evening of the 21st when the radio operator at the Soo reported that the steamer *Glenfinnan* last saw the "...*Lambton* at 2 p.m. on the 19th, forty miles out from Whitefish Point heading for Caribou Island." The following day the *Glenfinnan* reported that the Caribou Island Light was still not burning, a bad omen for the fate of the *Lambton*.

On April 23, a message was received by the Canadian Marine Agent at the Soo that the downbound Canadian steamer *Valcartier* reported that she hadn't seen the *Lambton*, but at 6:30 a.m., on the 20th, "about 25 miles southeast of Michipicoten Island and 15 miles east of Caribou, saw what looked like a top of a small pilothouse painted white, trimmed with bright red," and some additional wreckage. The wheelsman on the *Valcartier* had sailed the year before on the *Lambton* and he was sure it was her pilothouse. The area of the sighting was slightly off the normal vessel track.

No immediate action on the *Lambton* was initiated until the evening of April 23, when Mr. J.N. Arthurs, the Canadian Superintendent of Lights, returned to his home after placing light keepers at Griffith Island, Richards Landing and Shoal Island, all in the lower St. Marys River. Arthurs knew nothing of the missing *Lambton* until he arrived back at his home but he responded to the situation magnificently. He immediately contacted the Canadian authorities to authorize a full search, and took steps to arrange the charter of the big tug *G.R. Gray*, owned by the Lake Superior Paper Company. She was the only suitable vessel available fitted out for the season. If the *Lambton* was wrecked and her men marooned at some desolate north shore islet, every hour of delay could spell death. With Superintendent Arthurs and quickly obtained substitute lightkeepers aboard, the *Gray* departed the Soo at 6:30 p.m., to begin the search. Regardless of the fate of the *Lambton* he intended to try to get the lights into operation. Heavy pack ice encountered in Whitefish Bay forced her to reluctantly anchor off Point Au Pins on the Canadian shore and await the passage of an upbound freighter to break open a path. At 10:00 a.m., on the 25th, a steamer passed upbound and the *Gray* fell in behind, following in her wake to open water.

Passing Parisian Island in Whitefish Bay, Arthurs noted that neither the lighthouse nor the foghorn were operating. Since the ice was too thick to attempt a landing to investigate, the *Gray* continued to Whitefish Point, where Arthurs determined from the wireless operator that the Parisian Island light hadn't been seen this season. He could only surmise that the ice had also been too thick for the *Lambton* to land the lightkeepers. The *Lambton* would have continued on for Caribou Island, with the intention of stopping at Parisian Island on her way back to the Soo. The luckless Parisian Island men were forced to share the fate of the *Lambton*.

*The Lake Superior Paper Company tug G.R. GRAY decked out in holiday flags marking her arrival in the Soo in 1920.
Credit: Rutherford B. Hayes Presidential Center*

During the next five days the *Gray* thoroughly searched eastern Lake Superior. Not only did she investigate Caribou and Michipicoten Islands, but she also coasted the entire lakeshore from the Michipicoten River on the north shore south to Whitefish Bay and methodically cruised the open lake. The U.S. Coast Guard Cutter *Cook* assisted the search efforts by sweeping the south shore. Arthurs also alerted all area lightkeepers to keep a special watch for wreckage, and made persistent inquiries of commercial vessels. Someone must have seen something of his lost tug? "Where is the *Lambton*?"

To gain a better appreciation of the search effort made for the *Lambton*, this writer carefully plotted the movements of the *Gray* and those of assisting vessels, and made proper time notations for each. In examining the results, two facts become clear. First, that the tug made a painstaking search, and second, that Arthurs and the *Gray* were constantly on the move. It appears doubtful that Arthurs was able at any time to snatch more than an hour's nap.

Finally some more detailed reports trickled in to Authurs. On April 23, the steamer *Glenlivet* reported sighting the *Lambton* on the 19th, 40 miles above Whitefish Point. The steamer's crew could see the tug's steering gear was obviously disabled and she was steering with cables. The steamer *Osler* also reported sighting her on the 19th, approximately 40 miles above Whitefish Point and that the worst of the gale struck two hours later. The steamer *Westmount* reported nearly the same.

The most ominous sighting report was that of the *Midland Prince*. It stated that around noon of the 19th the steamer was in sight of the *Lambton*, but lost track of her during its battle with the rising gale. During the storm the wind shifted from southeast to northeast and setup one of the worst cross seas the steamer's officers had ever seen. When the gale passed, the *Lambton* was not in sight.

The steamer Midland Prince Credit: K.E. Thro

The *Glenfinnan's* captain reported that while the *Lambton*, *Glenfinnan* and *Glenlivet* were working their way through Whitefish Bay, his ship became stalled in the thick ice and the *Lambton* came to her assistance. In the process of breaking the large steamer free, the *Lambton* collided with her on her quarter. However, the *Glenfinnan's* master reported the *Lambton* received no damages. He also said that before the three vessels cleared the ice field, the *Lambton* broke her steering gear, and as a substitute, rigged one-inch lines directly to her rudder quadrant, without using relieving tackle.

The *Lambton* had a small Drake steam steering engine located in the pilothouse. The Drake meant the wheelsman did not move the wheel a full turn to turn the tug, but only far enough to open the valve and the gear would operate turning a drum taking the chain in until the rudder moved as needed. A turn of the wheel back, closed the valve and the engine stopped. One previous *Lambton*wheelsman remembered keeping her on course was no easy job. The Drake was a bit tricky to become used to using.

When Arthurs was able to examine all the meager evidence, he concluded that the three boats remained together until 2:00 p.m., when they were roughly 35 miles past Whitefish Point. There the weather began to threaten and the two Playfair boats returned to the shelter of Whitefish Point, arriving 10 minutes before the gale broke. The *Lambton*, however, forged on into the lake. Perhaps she was filled with an overdose of self-importance. She may have been a mere tug but carried on official business. Nothing should delay her in her important task!

Weather logs for the eastern Lake are all in agreement that on April 19, a northeast gale began approximately at 2:00 p.m. and reached a peak around 6:00 p.m., when Whitefish Point recorded a wind velocity of 60 miles per hour. Undoubtedly there were local variations. On the open lake it would have blown even more powerful.

Additional wreckage, undeniably that of the *Lambton*, was sighted by the steamer *Grant Morden* 14 miles northwest of Crisp Point on the Michigan coast. Later the steamer *Collingwood* ran through the same wreckage field.

From all available information, Superintendent Arthurs determined that the *Lambton* was lost about 6:00 p.m. on Wednesday the 19th, somewhere on a track between Caribou Island and Gargantua, Ontario. He believed that when the worst of the gale struck, the *Lambton* would have run for shelter at the north shore, especially since the gale seemed to come northeast. The *Lambton* foundered before reaching safety.

The *Lambton* was only 13 years old, and a seaworthy vessel. She was the same vessel that weathered gales before, why did she succumb that day? This writer thinks her foundering was a direct result of her "jury rigged" steering gear. Even in a small vessel it often takes two men to handle the wheel in a gale, but with only direct lines and no tackle rigged, it would be nearly impossible for the *Lambton* to hold her headway. She was a doomed vessel!

Some marine men blamed the loss on her open rudder quadrant which was exposed to freezing spray. It was bad enough that the crew sometimes had to chop the ice off it to prevent it from jamming. The lifeboats were also located on top of the pilothouse, a difficult position for the crew to reach in a storm.

To this day the *Lambton* remains "missing." Her wreck has never been found. She and her crew are a constant and tragic reminder of the dangers faced by those who "kept the lights."

References:

Appleton, Thomas, *Usque ad Mare, A History of the Canadian Coast and Marine Services* (Ottawa: Department of Transportation, 1968), pp. 250-252.

Appleton, Thomas, correspondence with author, November 11, 1977

Daily Mining Journal (Marquette, Michigan), April 25, 26, 1922.

Beaton, Horace L., *From the Wheelhouse, The Story of a Great Lakes Captain* (Cheltenham, Ontario: Boston Mills Press, 1979), pp. 12-13.

The Globe (Toronto, Ontario), April 24, 25, 27, 28, 1922.

Inches, H.C., *The Great Lakes Wooden Ship Building Era* (Vermilion, Ohio: Great Lakes Historical Society, 1976).

Mansfield, John B., *History of the Great Lakes, Volume I* (Chicago: J.H. Beers and Company, 1899).

Marine Collection. Rutherford B. Hayes Presidential Library, Fremont, Ohio.

Mills, John M., *Canadian Coastal and Inland Steam Vessels, 1809-1930* (Providence, Rhode Island: The Steamship Historical Society of America, 1979), pp. 69, 101.

Runge Collection, Wisconsin Marine Historical Society, Milwaukee, Wisconsin.

Transcript of Register, Canadian Lighthouse Tender LAMBTON.

Van der Linden, Reverend Peter, *Great Lakes Ships We Remember, II* (Cleveland, Ohio: Freshwater Press, 1984), 216.

The Rock and the Cox

The thick gray fog softly blanketed the rocky southern end of Isle Royale. It hung just above the water, giving and other worldly appearance right out of a science fiction movie. Beneath the curly-gray tendrils of cloud the lake was nearly flat. This supernatural aura was heightened by the masts of a large steamer moving eerily through the dense gray cotton.

High in his eight-story lighthouse, keeper John F. Soldenski paused to catch his breath after climbing the steep stairs to the galley. He had just finished a day of painting, something he had been

Lonely and desolate, Rock of Ages Reef lighthouse stands guard over the deadly shoal at the southwest lip of Isle Royale. Credit: U.S. Coast Guard

busy at all month! And he was getting a little tired of it! But regulations said paint the lighthouse every year, so paint he did. To take his mind off his endless task he stared out at the unearthly scene before him. Inexplicably the twin masts of the unknown steamer slowly turned until they lined up directly with the lighthouse. Soldenski frantically blew the fog whistle, but the strange steamer held her course seemingly oblivious to the warning. The appalled keeper watched the masts grow larger with each passing moment. The strange steamer struck Rock of Ages Reef between the light and the buoy with a shattering screech of torn steel. Soldenski could only think, "Damn it, what more could I have done? The whistle was blowing its standard pattern of a two-second blast every 28 seconds. I even overrode it and blew the danger signal! What more could I have done?"

First exhibited on October 26, 1908, Rock of Ages Light was one of the newest on the Great Lakes. Due to the remote location, its construction was considered a major engineering feat. It was intended to aid vessels to clear the rocks at the southwest end of Isle Royale. During the fall many ships bound to and from Duluth, Minnesota, or Superior, Wisconsin, sheltered from the strong west winds by steering a course along the Lake Superior north shore and in the lee of Isle Royale when the lake is too rough for a more southerly course. The lighthouse is located at the west end tip of Isle Royale, which is at the northwest corner of Lake Superior. The station is built on a rock 50 feet wide and 210 feet long, jutting a bare 16 feet above the water. The cylindrical tower is built of brick with concrete trim and a steel skeleton framework. The second order Fresnel lens, with a focal plane of 117 feet, flashed at an estimated 940,000 candlepower, visible on a clear day for a distance of 19 miles.

The story of this strange wreck really begins in 1901, Thirty-two years before the steamer hit the reef. It was then that the steamer *Puritan*, official number 150898, slid down the heavily greased ways of the Craig Shipyard at Toledo, Ohio, and first tasted fresh water. The Graham and Morton Transportation Company, was proud of its new vessel. When launched she measured 233 feet in length, 40 feet in beam, 26 feet in depth and 1,547 gross registered tons. Proving herself just a little too small, in 1908, she was lengthened to 259 feet, increasing her tonnage to 1,792. Until 1918, she made regular trips from Chicago to Michigan's Benton Harbor and St. Joseph with an occasional foray to Mackinac Island. All the while she carried happy vacationers in luxury and comfort.

In 1918 she was sold to the Michigan Transit Company and subsequently taken over by the United States Navy during World War I for services as a troop transport and training ship for new sailors. Reportedly she saw some service on the North Atlantic. The following year she returned to regular passenger service under the colors of the Chicago, Racine and Milwaukee Line. In 1933, the now veteran vessel was purchased by George M. Cox, a New Orleans lumber and shipping magnate. He found her in Manistee, Michigan, where she had been laid up for two years, a victim of the Depression. Cox promptly renamed her after himself.

Cox formed a new company, the Isle Royale Transit Company listing the *Cox* and the steamer *Isle Royale* as the principal assets. With the Century of Progress Exposition scheduled to open in Chicago, Cox believed his line would have no trouble finding passengers. *Cox* also intended to use the ship for weekend cruises from Chicago to Mackinac Island and other lake ports between. He planned to fill her with Rotarians, Lions and chamber of commerce groups out for lake excursions. He earnestly thought there would be no shortage of patrons. The larger *Isle Royale* (310 feet) would be used for the regular scheduled Chicago-Lake Superior passenger runs.

The *Isle Royale* was far more elaborate than the *Cox*, having accommodations for 400 passengers, an 80-by-30-foot dance floor, a large lounge and even a sports deck. A "first class" floor show with 10 women led by Fifi D'Orsay of film and vaudeville fame and a lively dance band were also featured.

The *Cox* was completely refurbished at a cost of $80,000, to include a coat of sparkling white paint for her hull and a sheen of black for her stack. New staterooms, cabins and other accommodations were also built on her upper deck to provide for the greatest number of paying passengers possible. On May 24, 1933, the glistening steamer left her Manistee dock for Chicago where she was given a great welcome and officially rechristened, *"George M. Cox"* by the vivacious daughter of the city's mayor. After both vessels were well established in the passenger and freight trade it was intended the larger *Isle Royale* would make the bulk of the long trips and the *Cox* stick to the occasional short excursion, staying mostly in Chicago as a sort of floating hotel.

Before leaving Manistee for the final time, George Cox gave an impromptu press conference, clearly stating his objectives for the new line. "The boats are elegantly equipped and everything that can possibly be done will be offered for the passenger's pleasure. The ships, however, are going to remain clean, there'll be no gambling or disorder if we have to sink them first." Considering the ultimate fate of the *Cox*, the temptation to speculate on what would really be going on is very tempting. At the time services of a very personal nature were common on many of the boats running out of Chicago. Often referred to in the polite press as "disorderly conduct," it was nothing of the kind. The women rotated from cabin to cabin in a very "orderly" fashion!

She left Chicago almost empty on her inaugural trip, intending to pick up a full load of 250 passengers at Thunder Bay, Ontario (Fort William-Port Arthur). A large dockside celebration, complete with brass band and top-hatted dignitaries, was planned at the Canadian lakehead. The 18 passengers that were already aboard were friends of the owner enjoying a "free ride." With such a light load of travelers the catering crew had a good chance to settle down their routine and learn their jobs. Her trip up Lakes Michigan and Superior and through the Keweenaw waterway was totally uneventful, a pleasant cruise for all aboard. But things were about to liven up.

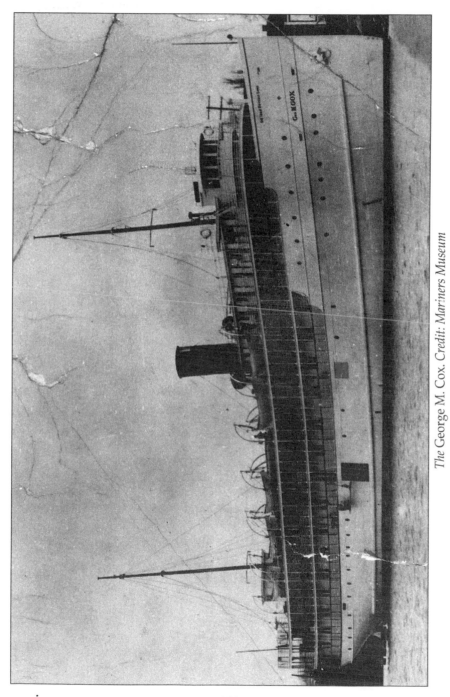

The George M. Cox. Credit: Mariners Museum

Later, during the welcoming ceremony at Houghton, Cox said, "Our boats are seaworthy, in first-class condition and we have spared no effort to provide the last word in comfort, luxury, service and entertainment." Again, the full nature of the entertainment available can be speculated.

At approximately 2:00 p.m., May 28, 1933, the *Cox* left Houghton, Michigan, and went on through to the Upper Entry at the western end of the waterway. Once in the open lake she increased shaft revolutions and set her course steady for Rock of Ages light, where she would turn to starboard for the run to Port Arthur. George Johnson, a veteran lake skipper from Traverse City, Michigan, was her captain. After assuring all was in order, Johnson turned the watch over to the first mate and went below. The steamer sped on at 17 miles per hour over the flat, gently undulating lake surface, her white bow foam matching the pristine hull. When the *Cox* started to run into patchy fog, the mate called the captain back to the bridge. Some witnesses said he reduced speed to 10 miles per hour. Other sources state the speed was not reduced. At some point both men sighted the top of Rock of Ages Light. As Soldenski was looking at them, they were apparently looking at him. Several passengers remembered even hearing the light's fog horn. As in other aspects of the wreck, there is also confusion when exactly she hit. George Cox claimed his watch said 6:31 p.m. Others on board stated 6:20 p.m. But hit she did, slamming into the rocks with incredible force.

Many of the guests had just been seated for the evening meal when the steamer struck the reef with a fearful crash. The *Cox's* orchestra was playing dreamy waltzes when the world seemed to collapse all around them. Fine crystal and service china shattered to the deck. Furniture slid down the compartment and crashed against bulkheads. Steaming trays of food flew into the air as stewards were unceremoniously thrown to the hard steel deck. Cries of the injured mingled with the loud roar of steam escaping from broken pipes ripped loose from their fittings by the force of the

The Cox on the rocks. Credit: Lake Superior Marine Museum

impact. Stunned passengers and crew picked themselves up and ran outside to see what had happened.

Initial reports indicated 50 people were injured in the crash, three of them seriously. One of the latter had a broken leg. Another was badly burned when a large vat of boiling fat for French fries overturned on him.

Adeline Keeling, the ship's 23-year-old nurse, described her experience: "There was one heavy thud, followed by a series of crashes. The passengers were at dinner at the time. . . I saw a heavy buffet table slide across the floor and crash into tables and a partition. I was in my stateroom and was thrown against a door and stunned. The stewardess, Beatrice Cole, helped me to my feet and was herself knocked down in the second crash. There was no panic, but the steamer listed heavily to port and the passengers and crew rushed to starboard. It was impossible to lower the starboard boats because of the list of the vessel, but the port boats were lowered and ferried us all to the lighthouse."

Keeling was considered one of the heroines of the wreck, working incessantly to comfort the injured and treat their wounds, both on the ship and later in the lighthouse. Since medical supplies to treat such a large number of causalities were nearly nonexistent, women's dresses and slips were torn into makeshift bandages.

After seeing the wreck or at least the reaction of the two masts to the ship hitting the reef and hearing the subsequent crash, Soldenski reacted as best he could. He launched the station's motor lifeboat and worked his way through the fog to the wreck. By the time he reached the *Cox*, the lifeboats were already in the water so he passed a tow line to them and brought them to the lighthouse.

The *Cox* had an estimated 110 feet of her white bow high in the air, like the canine tooth of a giant beast. Her aft was awash and she was listing approximately 40 degrees to port. The force of the crash ripped the engines from their moorings and water was flooding into the lower decks. The enormous force of the collision may

The Coast Guard cutter Crawford raced to the aid of the steamer! Credit: U.S. Coast Guard

have been a godsend. Had she been going slower and as a result struck the reef without sufficient power to keep her impaled, she could have quickly slid off and sank immediately. The death toll could have been very high indeed. The ship's wireless immediately began to tap out an SOS.

The Coast Guard Cutter *Crawford* was at her dock in Two Harbors, Minnesota, nearly 125 miles to the southwest and engaged in the normal Saturday routine. The quiet was shattered very quickly when the radio watch intercepted the SOS. The following are excerpts from the *Crawford's* log:

> *Midnight to 9:00 A.M.*
> Vessel moved to dock at Two Harbors, Minnesota. 6:00 call all hands. Crew carried out morning routine duties. Inspected magazine and powder samples condition, dry and normal. Warmed up main engine. 8:00 liberty party returned on time.
>
> *9:00 A.M. to 4:00 P.M*
> Vessel moored as before. Crew engaged in various duties about the vessel ... 11:20, inspection of ship and bedding, tested Flood Cock. 1:00 granted liberty to watch until 9:00 A.M. tomorrow.
>
> *4:00 P.M. to 8:00 P.M.*
> 6:00 received an intercepted message from S.S. *Morris Tremaine* (430-foot freighter) via Port Arthur, Ontario addressed to Coast Guard Station at Portage, Michigan, stating that steamer *George M. Cox* was on rocks in the vicinity of Rock of Ages Light and in need of immediate assistance. Passengers and crew were now abandoning ship ... 6:30 underway, proceeding to render assistance. 6:40, Two Harbors Light abeam ... 450 R.P.M. best possible speed.

8:00 P.M. to Midnight

8:20, Split Rock Light abeam ... Keeping in constant radio with *S.S. Morris Tremaine* throughout watch of conditions of *George M. Cox*. Was informed by master of MORRIS TREMAINE that he would remain in the vicinity of *Cox* until the arrival of *Crawford* and that it was too foggy to proceed to Port Arthur, Ontario. 1:00, Officer in Charge Instructed and authorized Engineer Officer to put additional weight on the governors to enable us to increase revolutions from 450 to 475 R.P.M.

Midnight to 4:00 A.M. Sunday, May 28

Vessel underway as before, partly clear to dense fog, light N.E. airs. On course ... proceeding at best possible speed, 475 R.P.M. with caution in view of dense fog with double lookout on bow. No attempt was made to reduce speed during the watch due to lives being at stake on the *George M. Cox*.

4:00 A.M. to 8.00 A.M.

standing towards Rock of Ages Light at 475 R.P.M. Vessel running on bearing of radio direction finder, there being magnetic attraction in this vicinity. It was not advisable to rely on compass course the last 15 miles. 5:10, picked up Rock of Ages fog signal dead ahead, reduced to half speed. 5:20, about a mile from light, reduced to slow speed. 5:30, Rock of Ages light 300 feet ahead, stopped. 5:35, anchored in 3 fathoms of water."

As the *Crawford* raced to the scene, the drama on the *Cox* continued. The message the *Crawford* had intercepted was ultimately delivered to the correct address, resulting in the hurried 6:10 a.m.

departure of the Portage Station lifeboat for the wreck. The Portage Coast Guard Station was on the Keweenaw Waterway, nearly 40 miles to the south of Isle Royale. Note that this was a delay of nearly 12 hours for the radio SOS to finally reach the station! There was additional delay when the motor lifeboat engine at first wouldn't start and once it did, it ran badly all the way to Isle Royale. When the lifeboat finally arrived at the *Cox* 2:15 p.m., it discovered that the passengers and crew had already been safely transferred to the lighthouse. All told, the lightkeeper and the *Cox's* crew removed 120 people (18 passengers and 102 crew) from the wreck. It was the largest mass rescue in Lake Superior history.

There was very little room in the lighthouse for anyone other than the assigned keepers. The tower had eight floors, not including the basement in the concrete crib. The upper levels offered poor shelter for the victims. The first floor contained the fog signal machinery and apparatus and the lifting engine for the crane on the open deck. A small office was on the second floor while the third had a miniature kitchen and mess room. The keeper and first assistant's quarters were on the fourth floor and second and third assistant's on the one above. The sixth and seventh floors contained the service room and watch room. The lamp room topped off the tower.

Throughout the long, cold night many survivors huddled together in the shelter of the lighthouse. It was too small to accommodate everyone inside so they took turns inside warming themselves. The survivors jammed into every nook and cranny of the structure, including the narrow and winding stairs up to the lamp room. Astoundingly, Beatrice Cole, the stewardess friend of nurse Keeling and injured in the collision, was carried up the stairs to an upper level using a mattress as an ad hoc stretcher. The cold of the Lake Superior spring was awful. The women from the ship were dressed only in light dresses and without coats. They shivered constantly in the cold night air. The members of the crew who were in their bunks when the steamer hit had abandoned her so quickly they only had their underclothes. The maids gallantly gave them their aprons to wrap around themselves for modesty. Later, talking to reporters, Cox said, "I can not say too much about the assistance rendered by the women at the lighthouse. In less than no time there was steaming coffee ready for the rescued and the atmosphere became more cherry." Regardless of good intentions, it is certain the unexpected guests devastated the lighthouse's meager food stock.

After the Portage lifeboat arrived at the light it was decided to shift 43 people to the Singer Hotel in Washington Harbor on Isle Royale, just eight miles away. At 4:30 a.m., the lifeboat started the transfer.

When finished ferrying the survivors to the hotel, the lifeboat, at the request of the master of the *Cox* and with assistance from the newly arrived Grand Marais (Minnesota) lifeboat, salvaged baggage from the stranded steamer.

At 6:30 a.m., the shift of passengers, crew and baggage from the light tower to the newly arrived *Crawford* began. By 7:50 a.m., the last of the bedraggled, tired and hungry survivors were brought aboard. The *Crawford* then made a short run in to Washington Harbor and embarked the passengers previously delivered there by the Portage lifeboat. At 9:45 a.m., the *Crawford* departed for Houghton.

Although no one was killed in the wreck, three crewmen were injured and they, with Mr. Cox and nurse Keeling, were taken to Port Arthur by the freighter *Morris Tremaine*. The *Cox* was a total loss of $150,000 (and had only been insured for $100,000).

In the official Report of Loss, Captain Johnson offers a clue to the cause of the *Cox* striking the reef. He stated, rather cryptically, that he took the steps of having "reduced to moderate speed and changing course from northwest to west after sound of siren of Rock of Ages Light becoming more distinct." This explained the turning maneuver seen by the lightkeeper. Since fog does tend to distort sounds, the error in turning towards, rather than away from the light, can also be explained. The report was a very neat document, offering no warning of the acrimony that would come when the principals met face-to-face at the inevitable government inquiry.

The official inquiry conducted at Houghton produced some remarkable testimony. The first mate, who had the watch from leaving Portage Entry to the actual point of impact, was accused by the captain of not steering the given course of northwest, one-half north. Although the mate violently denied the accusation, testimony by other crewmen corroborated the captain's charges. The mate had not steered the proper course!

Additional testimony charged the mate with deserting his post after colliding with the reef. One crew member said once first mate Kronk looked over the situation, he dashed off to his quarters and returned with a suit of clothes that he threw into a lifeboat before climbing in himself. Other witnesses said they saw him in a lifeboat rowing away from the *Cox* with only one woman passenger. The Captain, seeing the mate's light load, ordered him to return to the ship. The mate denied the charges, saying that he had stayed at his post until the very end and had assisted in launching several lifeboats before finally leaving himself. The second time though, he left he filled his boat with not one woman passenger but 17! This was generations before TV invented *Gilligan's Island*, but perhaps Kronk had been a reader of *Robinson Crusoe*. In any case, he seemed to think, "Well, if I am going to be shipwrecked I might as well make the best of it! I could be marooned here for a long, long time!"

Under heavy questioning the mate broke down and cried. After slamming his fist on the table in rage, he screamed that he was being "framed by a bunch of crooks!" He later engaged in a bout of fisticuffs with Captain Gilbert, the Vice President and Marine Superintendent of the line, when they met in the lobby of Houghton's Douglas House Hotel. The disaster proved too much for Captain Johnson. He retired from the lakes and never sailed again.

Evidence shows the mate's previous sailing record was not exactly a shining one. As the first mate of the steel steamer *Kiowa*, he was involved in one of the least honorable chapters of Lake Superior maritime history. The *Kiowa* had gone aground off Michigan's Au Sable Point in 1929 during a severe blizzard. Fearing the ship was about to break up in the waves, the captain led the way off her while brandishing a revolver and threatening his crew not to get in his way! Since the captain drowned in the storm, no punitive measures were taken against him; however, the mate lost his license for 90 days for his part in the debacle.

Although it has never been independently confirmed or placed in the official record, there is a revealing tale relating to the general state of sobriety aboard the *Cox*. Reportedly, when she passed through the Soo, she had trouble even getting into the lock. During the operation, one of the crew told a dock worker that everyone aboard was drunk and that he was leaving when she reached Houghton. If the crewman actually did jump ship, it was certainly a wise precaution showing excellent judgment.

When all the shouting, squabbling and backstabbing was finished, the entire affair is best summarized by the Rock of Ages lightkeeper's terse entry in his log for May 29: "Cleaning up the mess which was made." Once that was finished, Soldenski knew it was back to painting, the job that never ended.

While the *Cox* was on the rocks, salvage efforts, both official and unofficial, were made. The Thunder Bay tug *Strathmore* with the barge *Strathbuoy* recovered all moveable equipment and personal belongings of the passengers and crew, including two brand-new 1933 automobiles owned by George M.Cox.

For nearly a year the steamer stayed on the reef. All the while local fishermen boarded the *Cox* and stripped her of anything of value. The *Cox* was so badly damaged by the stranding that recovery of the vessel was never seriously considered. During an October gale, the remains of the shattered steamer broke in two and slipped off the reef.

The *Cox* may be all gone, but Rock of Ages light, just as its name-sake, persevered. Men continued to keep the old light until 1978, when it was finally automated. Like other remote lights, modern Coast Guardsmen looked on assignment there as a form of punishment. Automating the remote stations became not only a budget issue, but a morale one as well.

Some keepers of the old Lighthouse Service often sought assignment to the isolated stations. The pay was better and rotation shorter. There was also little opportunity to spend your money on a rock. Being cooped up on some desolate island wasn't so bad either, once you became used to it. One keeper at Stannard's Rock spent 99 consecutive days on it and emerged none the worse for the experience.

Today things are far different at Rock of Ages than when Soldenski stood his watch. If another steamer heads smack into the deadly reef, there is no keeper to watch in horror, just a couple of seagulls perched on the galley handrail. Before the men came and built the big tower the seagulls sat on the rock. Their view is better now, but what else has changed?

References:

Annual Reports, U. S. Lighthouse Service, 1896 - 1911.

Brown, Russell W., "Ships at Port Arthur and Fort William." *Inland Seas* (October, 1945).

Daily Mining Gazette (Houghton, Michigan). May 28,29,30; June 1, 9,17, 1933; May 27, 1983.

Duluth News-Tribune. July 25, 1976.

Fort William Daily Times Journal. May 29,30,31, June 2, 1933.

Frederikson, A.C. *Ships and Shipwrecks in Door County, Volume II* (Sturgeon Bay, Wisconsin: Door County Publishing Company, 1963).

Holden, Thom, "A Maiden Voyage Into History," Telescope (January-February 1984), pp. 3-10

Holden, Thom, "Wicks, Wrecks and Wilderness," *Inland Seas* (Summer 1997), pp. 137-139.

Journal of the Light Station at Rock of Ages. May 1933, RG 26, NARA.

Lake Carrier's Association, *Annual Report of the Lake Carrier's Association, -* 1933, pp. 34-37.

Log of the Coast Guard Patrol Boat Crawford. May 1933, RG 26, NARA.

"Official Dispatches, U.S. Coast Guard", May 28, June 20, July 19,1933, RG 26, NARA.

National Archives and Records Service, correspondence with author, September 12, 27, October 1, 1973.

Nelson, Donald L., correspondence with author, n.d.

New York Times, May 28, 29, 1933.

Report of Casualty, George M. Cox. July 20,1933, RG 26, NARA.

Rock of Ages Light," [*http://www.cr.nps*.gov/history/maritime/rockages.html] January 12, 1997.

Superior Evening Telegram (Superior, Wisconsin). May 27, 1983.

U.S. Coast Guard, correspondence with author concerning wreck of *George M. Cox*, June 3. July 13, 16. 20, 27, 28, October 16, 1933.

U.S. Department of Commerce, Bureau of Navigation. "Consolidated Certificate of Enrollment and License, Steamer GEORGE M. COX." 1932.

Van der Linden, Reverend Peter, ed. *Great Lakes Ships We Remember*, (Cleveland: Freshwater Press, 1979).

Wolff, Julius F., "A Lake Superior Lifesaver Reminisces." *Inland Seas*, (Summer, 1968).

The Lighthouse

It is often said that ships have a spirit, a soul, a living aspect to them. Whether built of steel, wood or even fiberglass, there is an essence within the physical structure. A good captain lets the ship talk to him and takes note of what it says.

I believe a lighthouse has the same type of spirit and it too can speak to the keeper. There are cases where the old-time wickies claimed their lights did talk to them, telling of their fears and desires. And the keepers spoke back to the lights, reassuring them when the gales blew hard and encouraging them to keep the light burning. Like ships, lights were always feminine, never masculine.

This tale is about the most famous shipwreck in modern Great Lakes history and the lighthouse that witnessed it. While obviously fictional in some respects, it is essentially true. It also puts a different spin on the terrible tragedy.

The icy wind blew out of the northwest with incredible force. The old skeletal tower shook and rattled. Every ounce of strength the designers planned into her was stressed to the limit. As she did so many times before, she passed the test. Originally, way back in 1849, a rough stone tower did the same job. Construction, however, was of poor quality and with the boom in lake commerce it was plain a taller tower was needed. Rather than rebuild the stone one, the Lighthouse Board tore it down and in its place erected one of the iron skeletal towers that were then the rage, especially for areas where good foundations could not be found. In 1861 the contractor arrived on site and within a matter of months the job was done. The new 76-foot tower had a big Fresnel lens that directed its beam 17 miles out into the dark lake. Everyone - sailors, fishermen and lighthouse men - all agreed it was a great improvement over the old light.

The new tower survived the worst the big lake could throw at her. Rain battled against her thick lamp room windows, snow drifted 20 feet deep across the keeper's house and sleet ricocheted off

175

The iron tower at Whitefish Point stands strong and proud against the raw power of Lake Superior. Credit: Author's Collection

the iron legs. Deep thunder rolled overhead and lightning flashed across the sky. Sometimes the tower fairly hummed with static electricity. But it was the wind, always the appalling wind that she feared the worst. Spawned deep in an arctic hell, its predominant direction was from the northwest. Screaming down over 180 miles of open water, it smashed into the tower so hard the structure trembled with the unseen force. The tower always withstood the onslaught, but sometimes it was a near thing, or at least so the keeper thought.

The men who kept the light were good workers. Day after day, for what seemed like an eternity, they loyally performed the countless thankless tasks it took to keep her running at peak efficiency. Often they spoke to the tower, especially during the long night watches. Sometimes it was just patting a hand against a cold metal pedestal, or a kind word during an especially violent storm. She spoke back too, reassuring them, telling them it was OK; she could stand up to the blasts and fury of the gale. She was certain the men understood her.

From their vantage high in the lantern room the keepers could watch far out into the lake. The light watched too. Sometimes in the summer not a ripple broke the surface. During the height of fall gales waves the size of two-story houses marched down the lake sweeping all before.

Through the decades the old tower had seen it all. Summer's warmth and winter's icy cold; spring's chilly promise and fall's deadly storms. The worst of course was the fall, when the horrendous storms wreaked such havoc.

The light's job was to save ships, to keep them clear of damage, warning them away from danger by the friendly beams of the big Fresnel. But storm was an enemy the light could not combat. Knowing that simple fact didn't make it any easier when the ships died, overwhelmed by wind and wave and the lifeless bodies of the crews littered the beaches. It tore at the light's guts.

She remembered every disaster. In November 1872, planets died when the schooner-barges *Saturn* and *Jupiter* perished off Gros Cap taking all 15 souls to their death, including the woman cook. September 1887 saw the schooner-barge *Niagara* overpowered by a howling northwester. Her crew escaped in the yawl moments before their ship sank, only to be swallowed by the grasping waves. The light heard the anguished cry from the big steel steamer *Cyprus*, barely 21 days out of the builder's yard when she broke in two in October 1907. All people aboard except one man died with her. A year later the steel steamer *D. M. Clemson*, ravaged by another fall monster, perished with all hands.

The old light knew them all and so many more. It heard the dreadful sounds of splintering wood and ripping steel. And the appalling shrieks of the men and women as they sank forever beneath the cold water.

Sailors had long called this area the "Graveyard of the Lakes." More good ships and crews met their end in these waters than anywhere else. The light was aware that only she heard these ungodly sounds, never her keepers. They only learned of the catastrophes from the inevitable wreckage that washed ashore. She knew long before and grieved for every soul lost, for their wives, sons and daughters left behind. Dying was easy; it's the keeping on living that's hard.

As time passed such tragedies became fewer and fewer. The ships grew in size and were less affected by wind and sea. New devices like RDF (Radio Direction Finder), *Loran* (Long Range Navigation) and radar helped them keep a true course and steer clear of rocks and shoals.

The terrible wind still blew hard and wild and the tower, now older but as strong as ever, still shook in the icy blasts. Out on the ferocious lake no ships were sinking or human beings dying. Not any more. Not now.

Then came the storm. She hadn't seen anything like it for a long, long time. The one in November 1913 was probably as bad; maybe even the 1940 Armistice Day storm was an equal. However, it had been such a long time it was impossible to judge.

It began innocently enough. November 9, 1975 was a beautiful day, calm and warm, unusual for the fall on Lake Superior and a welcome contrast to the normal cold rain and blustery winds. During night the wind went to gale force from the northeast. This meant wind speeds of 39-46 miles per hour. It would be tough going for sailors but the big new ships could handle the weather alright. Then the wind increased in intensity to storm force, 55-63 miles per hour, still from the northeast. Later the winds blew harder still, beyond where men on a ship could measure the speed. Some sailors claimed a speed of 100 miles per hour! In the afternoon the winds backed northwest and huge waves piled up, roaring down from the Canadian lakehead unchecked for 180 miles.

Now it was hell for the sailors, regardless of the size of the vessel. Some waves crested at better than 30 feet, huge mountains of moving water crushing all in their path.

The dreadful wind slashed at everything it could. Ripping shingles off the abandoned keeper's house and wrenching trees out of the ground. Other trees snapped like matchsticks. Again and again, the iron tower vibrated from the storming fingers of wind. As always it stood firm and strong. Perhaps one day the wind would finally win the eternal fight, but not today, not this storm.

Mountainous waves of gray water slammed into the sloping beach washing over the old wood breakwater and ran high up on the shore. Occasionally, a wave broke through the dunes and ran surging down the rough county road. The shifting wind set up a vicious cross-chop, when the waves bounced off the rock-bound Canadian shore and back into the lake. On the open water there was no rhyme or reason to the seas. First this way, then that way. The lake had become a true maelstrom!

The men that kept the light were long gone, dismissed in the name of efficiency. Since 1970, she ran on automatic. Machines did the work the old wickies used to do. As if by magic the light came on at dusk and flickered off at dawn. If a bulb burned out, a machine whirled and it was automatically replaced with a new bulb. When the gray tendrils of fog enveloped the water, the big horn started its mournful blare on its own volition. It was all so easy. It was all automatic!

Of course, no one cut the grass or polished her brass. No one carefully dusted the lamp room, painted or cleaned. The big Fresnel was gone too, replaced with a tiny plastic "optic" that insulted the light keeper's art. The men and their families that injected their life into the lighthouse were gone, too. No children played on the wide lawn or splashed in the water. When Christmas came there were no trees bright with shiny ornaments. Still the venerable light refused to die. She lived on. As long as she had a purpose she would live. And that damned little plastic lens provided her purpose!

The men that installed the new automated systems made a horrendous, inexcusable error. They ran the thin wires that controlled the new automatic machinery on telephone poles. Up from the main line to the lonely lighthouse station, the wires dangled from wooden cross arms nailed to wooden poles. The wind attacked the poles with a vengeance, knocking several to the ground and snapping the vulnerable wires, stopping the automatic machinery dead. The light went black. No warning light beamed out from the old tower, nor radio beacon signal from the nearby antenna. Worse, the generator that was supposed to automatically kick in, failed. It sat cold and quiet, a useless piece of gray machinery. The missing beam embarrassed the old light acutely. But she was also used to the feeling since it had happened many times before, since the men had automated her. Still, it wounded her deeply. The light longed for the old days when her keepers never let the light go out. Not once! Not for any reason! Not ever!

She sensed that something very bad was happening, something far out on the lake, beyond her vision. Although she had not had this feeling for a long time, there was no mistaking the gut-wrenching dread that over came her. There was a ship in trouble, very severe trouble.

She didn't know if her light would make a difference but she tried to will her beam back on; to make it glow by pure force of desire. It was no good. Without the magic of the thin wires she was just a dark and useless hunk of iron!

Her special sense, developed from so many years of faithful service, continued to "tell" her of a drama far off shore, in the heart of the raging tempest. The big freighter was heading downbound for "her" point and deeply laden with ore. She was running unusually low in the water. Something was plainly wrong. Green waves regularly swept down the length of the open spar deck, crashing into the steel wall aft of her Texas. Blinding snow squalls plunged her into a world of white, then moved on up the lake. The light could sense fear in the pilothouse. Although the men were scared, there was no panic. They were professional mariners as good as ever sailed the lakes, long used to danger. Nonetheless, there was an undercurrent of fear. They knew something was wrong!

The old light felt the ship was injured, that she had gutted herself on one of Superior's innumerable deepwater shoals. Perhaps it was the spirit of the ship in silent communication with that of the light, sisters together in the terrible storm. The ship only held herself to together by supreme effort. Her steel sinews struggled mightily to overcome the torn bottom. The men knew their ship was hurt, just not how bad. They, too, willed her to continue. "Come on girl! Just one more mile, then another after that! You can do it!"

Too proud to radio for help, there was nothing anyone could do anyway. The men grimly held to their course to try to tuck in behind Whitefish Point. Perhaps there, in the shelter of the land, they could slide the ship smoothly on a gentle sand bottom and all would be safe.

It was then the light saw it, several miles behind the ship and moving fast on an identical track. A huge wall churning of water, a wave building ever larger as it approached the stern of the steamer. Moving and surging with increasing strength, it was almost a living creature, bent on the destruction of all in its path. Within minutes it struck the big freighter, breaking hard on the aft cabin, thundering through the lifeboat covers and partially ripping the boats clear of the davits. Thundering down the length of the deck it smashed into the stern of the pilothouse with pile driver force. The overwhelming weight of the water collapsed the forward hatches and flooded into the number one and two cargo holds. Pushed down by the added weight of the wave, the bow suddenly dove for the bottom. A wall of water exploded through the pilothouse windows, instantly killing the men on watch. Continuing the downward plunge the bow knifed into the lake bottom, plowing a deep furrow in the mud. The bow's dive sent the stern high above the waves where for a second it lingered, before following the bow down to the bottom of the lake. Just after disappearing from view the colossal torque wrenched the stern third of the ship off from the rest.

The storm ruled the lake above. Beneath the surface though, all was deadly quiet. The forward third of the freighter sat upright, great swirls of mud still settling silently about her from the impact with the bottom. The stern third was upside down several hundred feet away. The middle third was represented by the pile of rubble in between, the result of the wrenching breakup.

The light heard the scream, the overpowering primitive howl of both ship and crew when life was viciously snatched away. There was no doubt everyone was gone, in a flash, in an instant. There was no desperate struggling in the water, slowly tiring and drowning or freezing to death in a lifeboat. Just near instant death. At least it was merciful, if death could ever be so described. In the storm-blown waters above two battered lifeboats drifted as did two life rafts. The light knew all were empty. There would be weeping on the lakes tonight and tomorrow and for months to come. As in the days of old, families would cry for the fathers and sons taken by Superior.

Although she told herself her missing light played no role in the tragedy, in her heart she could not be certain. There was doubt! Maybe if the light or her RDF transmitter was on, the captain would have done something different, something that would have prevented the loss of ship and crew. The light had overheard two of the men on the bridge asking where the light was. Why couldn't they see it? Curse the fools who took away her keepers and took away her light!

When the news of the catastrophe became known people crowded her beach to look out into the gray and unforgiving lake. Trucks and cars filled her small parking lot and lined the road approaching it. Even a helicopter flew by overhead and later landed nearby for fuel. The men came and fixed the wires so the little plastic light shown again and the RDF emitted its invisible signal. All she could think though, was it was too little and too late. The damage was done.

Gradually the great storm blew itself out and the lake returned to normal. Several days later a long, thin object washed ashore. Dirty orange in color, it had a stenciled name on it, "S. S. *Edmund Fitzgerald.*" So that was the name of the ship! The light had seen her many times rounding the point. She would see her no longer. Now she was just one more ship the light had seen die; one of so many!

Bibliography

Books

Adamson, Hans Christian. *Keepers of the Lights.* New York: Greenberg, 1955.

Appleton, Thomas. *Usque ad Mare, A History of the Canadian Coast and Marine Services.* Ottawa: Department of Transportation., 1968.

Beaton, Horace L. *From the Wheelhouse, the Story of a Great Lakes Captain.* Cheltenham, Ontario: Boston Mills, 1979.

Bowen, Dana Thomas. *Memories of the Lakes.* Cleveland, Ohio: Freshwater Press, 1969.

Capron, Captain Walter C. *The U.S. Coast Guard.* New York: Franklin Watts, Inc., 1965.

De Wire, Elinor. *Guardians of the Lights: The Men and Women of the U.S. Lighthouse Service.* Sarasota, Florida: Pineapple Press, 1995.

Flint, Willard. *Lightships of the United States Government, Reference Notes.* Washington, DC: Coast Guard Historian's Office, 1989.

Frederickson, A.C. *Ships and Shipwrecks in Door County, Volume II* (Sturgeon Bay, Wisconsin: Door County Publishing Company, 1963.

Harris, Patrica Gruse. *New Buffalo, MI Lighthouse, 1839-1859.* Michigan City, Indiana: GEN-HI-LI, 1993.

Hirthe, Walter M. and Mary K. *Schooner Days in Door County.* Minneapolis, Minnesota: Voyager Press, 1986.

Holland, Francis Ross Jr. *America's Lighthouses, An Illustrated History.* New York: Dover Publications, 1988.

Holland, Hjalmar R. *Old Peninsula Days, Tales and Sketches of The Door Peninsula.* Madison, Wisconsin: Wisconsin House, 1972.

Inches, H. C. *The Great Lakes Wooden Shipbuilding Era.* Vermilion, Ohio: Great Lakes Historical Society, 1976.

Johnson, Arnold B. *The Modern Lighthouse Service.* Washington, DC: 1890.

Johnson, Robert Erwin. *Guardians of the Sea, History of the United States Coast Guard, 1915 to the Present.* Annapolis, Maryland: Naval Institute Press, 1987.

Knudsen, Arthur and Evelyn. *A Gleam Across the Wave*. nd.

Kozma, LuAnn Gaykowski. *Living at a Lighthouse, Oral Histories From the Great Lakes*. Great Lakes Lighthouse Keepers Association, 1987.

Lake Carrier's Association. *Annual Report of the Lake Carrier's Association - 1933*.

Law, William H. *Among the Lighthouses of the Great Lakes*. Detroit: W.H. Law, 1908.

Mansfield, John B. *History of the Great Lakes, Volume I*. Chicago: J.H. Beers and Company, 1899.

Mills, John M. *Canadian Coastal and Inland Steam Vessels, 1809-1930*. Providence, Rhode Island: The Steamship Historical Society of America, 1979.

National Maritime Initiative. *1994 Inventory of Historic Light Stations*. Washington, DC: US Department of the Interior, National Park Service, 1994.

New Buffalo Story, 1834-1976. New Buffalo, Michigan: New Buffalo Area Bicentennial Committee, 1976.

Penrose, Laurie. *A Traveler's Guide to 100 Eastern Great Lakes Lighthouses*. Davison, Michigan: Freide Publications, 1994.

Putnam, George R. *Lighthouses and Lightships of the United States*. New York: Houghton Mifflin Company, 1917.

Talbot, Frederick A. *Lightships and Lighthouses*. Philadelphia: J.B. Lippincott, 1913.

Townsend, Robert B. *Tales From The Great Lakes*. Toronto, Ontario: Dundurn Press, 1995.

Treasure Ships of the Great Lakes. Detroit: Maritime Research and Publishing, 1981.

Van der Linden, Reverend Peter J., ed. *Great Lakes Ships We Remember*. Cleveland, Ohio: Freshwater Press, 1979.

———— ed. *Great Lakes Ships We Remember II*. Cleveland, Ohio: Freshwater Press, 1984.

Vent, Myron H. *South Manitou Island*. New York: Publishing Center for Cultural Resources, 1980.

Weiss, George. *The Lighthouse Service, It's History, Activities and Organization*. Baltimore: The Johns Hopkins Press, 1916.

Whittle, D. W. ed. *Memoir of P.P. Bliss*. nd.

Woodford, Arthur M. *Charting the Inland Seas*. U.S. Corps of Engineers, 1991.

Government Documents

Dominion of Canada. Notice to Mariners, No. 54 of 1930.

Dominion of Canada. *Transcript of Register*, Canadian Lighthouse Tender *Lambton*.

Fairport International Exploration v. The Shipwrecked Vessel, *et al.*, No. 95-1783, 6 Cir. Ct. (1997).

Fairport International Exploration v. The Shipwrecked Vessel, Capt. Lawrence, No. 95-1783, Crt of App, 6 Cir. Ct., 1997.

"Journal of the Light Station at Rock of Ages." Record Group 26, National Archives and Records Administration (NARA), May 1933.

"Log of the Coast Guard Patrol Boat *Crawford*." RG 26, NARA, May 1933.

Lighthouse Letters Book, RG 26, NARA.

"Official Dispatches," U.S. Coast Guard, May 28, June 20, July 19, 1933, RG 26, NARA.

Register of Lighthouse Keepers, RG 26, NARA.

"Report of Casualty, *George M. Cox*." July 20, 1933, RG 26. NARA.

Transport Canada. *Annual Report of the Department of Marine, 1931*.

U.S. Department of Commerce, Bureau of Navigation. "Consolidated Certificate of Enrollment and License, Steamer *George M. Cox*." 1932, RG 26, NARA.

U.S. Department of Commerce. *United States Coast Pilot - 6, Great Lakes: Lakes Ontario, Erie, Huron, Michigan and Superior and St. Lawrence River*. Washington, DC: Government Printing Office, 1986.

U.S. Department of Commerce, Lighthouse Service. *The United States Lighthouse Service, 1915*. Washington, DC: Government Printing Office, 1916.

U.S. Department of the Treasury. *Annual Reports of the Lighthouse Board*. Government Printing Office, RG 26, NARA, various issues.

U.S. Department of the Treasury. *Annual Report of the Life-Saving Service, 1893*. Government Printing Office, RG 26, NARA, 1894.

Internet Sources

"A Brief History of Canadian Lighthouses," [*http://members.aol*.com/ stiffcrust/pharos/index.html#imperial]. November 5, 1997.

"Canada's Georgian Bay," [*http://www.biddeford*.com/lhdigest/ sept96/georgia.html]. October 28, 1997.

Columbus Dispatch (Columbus, Ohio). [*http://www.treasure*.com:80/ 20296.htm].

Grand Rapids Press (Grand Rapids, Michigan). [*http://www.treasure*.com/ 80/n19.htm], March 9, 1997.

Great Lakes Shipwreck. [*http://www.treasure*.com/80/n1,htm]. "Rock of Ages Light." [*http://www.cr.nps*.gov/history/ maritime/rockages.html], January 12, 1997.

Periodicals

Barada, Bill. "The Treasure of Poverty Island." *Skin Diver Magazine*. March 1969.

Biggs, Jerry. "Squaw Island." *Beacon*. December, 1995.

Farrant, Don. "Five Against the Lake." *Lighthouse Digest*. May, 1997.

Gilmartin, ET1 Joseph P. Sr. (Ret.). "The Keeper's Light." *Shipmates*. October, 1994.

Hawkins, Bruce. "A Miserable Piece of Work." *Michigan History*. July/August 1989.

Holden, Thom. "A Maiden Voyage Into History." *Telescope*. January/February, 1984.

Holden, Thom. "Wicks, Wrecks and Wilderness." *Inland Seas*. Summer, 1997.

Inland Seas. Summer, 1995; Spring, 1997; Summer, 1997.

Landon, Fred. "The Discovery of Superior Shoal." *Inland Seas.* Spring, 1959.

"Memorial For Six Coast Guardsmen Lost in 1942 is Long Overdue." *On Scene*, Spring, 1997.

Nelson, Donald L. "Lansing Shoal Lighthouse and the 1940 Armistice Day Storm." *Beacon*. September 1996.

Newsletter. Association for Great Lakes Maritime History, May, 1993.

Nor'Easter. July/August, 1994,

O'Donnell, Bob. "The Last Word." *Association for Great Lakes Maritime History Newsletter*. September/October, 1995.

Parsons, Captain R. W. "The Storm of 1940." *Inland Seas*. Spring, 1996.

Van Hoey, Mike. "Lights of the Straits." *Michigan History Magazine*, September/October, 1986.

Vinette, T.D. "Search For Gold: 1936, Poverty Island Passage." *Soundings*. nd.

Wolff, Julius F. "A Lake Superior Lifesaver Reminisces." *Inland Seas*. Summer, 1968.

Correspondence

Thomas Appleton to author, November 11, 1977.

Canadian Hydrographic Service to author.

Environment Canada to author, March 29, 1976.

Mrs. Dorathea F. Larsen to author, April 20, May 6, 1994.

National Archives and Records Service to author, September 12, 27; October 1, 1973.

Donald L. Nelson to author, March 9, 1996.

Donald L. Nelson to author, n.d.

U.S. Coast Guard, June 3; July 13, 13, 20, 27, 28; October 16, 1933.

U.S. Department of Commerce to author, May 23, 1973.

Newspapers

Action Shopper (Marquette, Michigan). September 14, 1981.

Daily Mining Gazette (Houghton, Michigan). May 28-30; June 1, 9, 17, 1933; May 27, 1983.

Duluth New-Tribune. July 25, 1976.

Fort William Daily Times Journal (Fort William, Ontario). May 29-31; June 2, 1933.

The Globe (Toronto, Ontario). April 24-28, 1922.

Great Lakes Log. May 1, July 1, 1995.

Milwaukee Journal (Milwaukee, Wisconsin). October 30, 1994.

Mining Journal (Marquette, Michigan). April 25-26, 1922; November 11, December 18, 1994.

New York Times. May 28-29, 1933.

Palladium-Times (Oswego, New York). December 3-5, 7-10, 1942.

Sacramento Bee (Sacramento, California). March 10, 1997.

Superior Evening Telegraph (Superior, Wisconsin). May 27, 1983.

Toronto Telegraph (Toronto, Ontario). August 26, 1933.

Upper Peninsula Sunday Times (Marquette, Michigan). July 29, 1979.

Collections

Hanson, Robert C. "Discovery of Superior Shoal." unpublished manuscript.

Author's Collection, Squaw Island.

Runge Collection, Wisconsin Marine Historical Society, Milwaukee, Wisconsin.

Rutherford B. Hayes Presidential Library, Fremont, Ohio.

Ivan Walton Collection, Bentley Historical Library, University of Michigan.

Interviews

Captain Edward Beganz, nd.

Mr. Louis Bauchan, March 5, 1997.

Mr. Richard Bennett, November 10, 1997.

Mr. T.D. Vinette, January 22, 1998.

ABOUT THE AUTHOR

FREDERICK STONEHOUSE holds a Master of Arts Degree in History from Northern Michigan University, Marquette, Michigan, and has authored six books on Great Lakes maritime history. *Isle Royale Shipwrecks, Went Missing, Munising Shipwrecks, Lake Superior's "Shipwreck Coast," Keweenaw Shipwrecks, The Wreck of the Edmund Fitzgerald* and *Dangerous Coast: Pictured Rocks Shipwrecks* are all published by Avery Color Studios.

He has also been a consultant for both the U.S. National Park Service and Parks Canada.

His articles have been published in *Skin Diver, Great Lakes Cruiser Magazine* and *Lake Superior Magazine*. He is a member of the Great Lakes Historical and Marquette County Historical Societies, the Lake Superior Marine Museum Association, the Marquette Underwater Preserve Committee, a member of the Board of Directors of the Marquette Maritime Museum and a member of the Board of Directors of the United States Life-Saving Service Heritage Association.

Other Fred Stonehouse titles
by Avery Color Studios, Inc.

- The Wreck of the Edmund Fitzgerald
- Dangerous Coast (Co-Author)
- Lake Superior's Shipwreck Coast
- Went Missing

Avery Color Studios, Inc. has a full line of Great Lakes oriented books, shipwreck and lighthouse maps, and lighthouse posters.

For a full color catalog call:

1-800-722-9925

Cover Photo: Big Tub, located on
Lake Huron. (Ont) Lighthouse Point on
Big Tub Harbour, west entrance to Tobermory.